THE JAGUAR XKs
The 1950s Pacesetters from Coventry

John Nikas

Photography by Marc Vorgers

AMBERLEY

First published 2018

Amberley Publishing
The Hill, Stroud
Gloucestershire, GL5 4EP

www.amberley-books.com

Copyright © John Nikas, 2018
Photographs copyright © Marc Vorgers

The right of John Nikas to be identified as the
Author of this work has been asserted in
accordance with the Copyright, Designs and
Patents Act 1988.

ISBN 978 1 4456 7346 2 (print)
ISBN 978 1 4456 7347 9 (ebook)

British Library Cataloguing in Publication Data.
A catalogue record for this book is available from
the British Library.

Typeset in 10pt on 13pt Celeste.
Origination by Amberley Publishing.
Printed in the UK.

Contents

Chapter 1
Flight of the Swallow

Following wounds received while serving in the Cheshire Yeomanry during the First World War, William Walmsley passed the first few years after the Armistice riding across the countryside on an ex-Army Triumph motorcycle, hoping to put the horrors of trench warfare on the Western Front out of his mind.

Inventive by nature and displaying a strong entrepreneurial bent, he earned money building simple but fashionable sidecars in a garden shed located behind the family home. In a time when the motorcycle was still the dominant form of transportation, though the motorcar was on the rise, sidecars were a popular means to increase their practicality by allowing the carriage of a passenger.

The son of a prosperous coal merchant in Cheshire, Walmsley had eschewed his father's trade, content to earn a few pounds from servicing motorcycles for local riders and building sidecars subject to the occasional custom order. Perhaps having experienced too much of life beyond his control, Walmsley was happy with his career choice. Frustrated with his inability to convince any other relatives to assume control of his coal operation, much less his son, Walmsley's father sold the business and his house in 1921, and moved everyone to the seashore in Blackpool.

Fortunately, the family's new residence at No. 23 King Edward Avenue had a large garage, where Walmsley immediately set up shop reconditioning war surplus Triumph motorcycles and building sidecars in greater numbers. Rather than fashion sidecars solely as a practical venture, Walmsley built his creations with an inimitable sense of style using an ash frame and polished octagonal aluminium panels for the bodies.

By late summer, working alongside his new bride – who handled the upholstery and some light trimming – Walmsley had cultivated a steady supply of customers and was soon completing a new sidecar every week. The first prototype, which Walmsley had built for his own use, was nicknamed 'Ot-as-Ell,' but the moniker was deemed much too risqué for public consumption. Instead, he chose the name 'Swallow' since the bird was known as a fast flyer despite its small size.

Walmsley, however, was not the only motorcycle fan in the neighbourhood. Across the street lived a twenty-year-old fellow enthusiast named William Lyons. Like Walmsley, Lyons had declined to follow his father's example in business, finding his piano trade rather less exciting than wheeled machinery. After a short apprenticeship at Crossley Motors proved personally unfulfilling, Lyons took a position selling cars for a local agent that represented Sunbeam.

Not long after the Walmsley family had moved to the coast, Lyons glimpsed a sidecar in his neighbour's yard and sauntered over for a look. Impressed with the stylish lines and obvious build quality, the youngster ordered one immediately. After taking delivery of his new prize, Lyons found that it attracted considerable attention from fellow riders and onlookers alike. Such interest was more than an idle curiosity, since he felt it showed the commercial potential in Walmsley's sidecars.

William Lyons sits astride a Harley-Davidson motorcycle in 1922. (Jaguar Land Rover Heritage)

Williams Lyons seated snugly in a Swallow sidecar alongside William Walmsley. (Jaguar Land Rover Heritage)

Lyons soon met with Walmsley, telling him that a viable business could be formed if production could be increased to around ten units per week. Although the statement met with some initial incredulity, Walmsley decided that the brash youngster had a point after some further consideration and a closer examination of the prospective finances involved. Somewhat surprisingly, both fathers supported their sons in this endeavour, seeing that they had a talent for the business, as well as enthusiasm.

With some backing from their respective families in the form of a £1,000 bank guarantee, the pair started their business, operating from a small workshop located on Bloomfield Road, near the south side of town. Formal establishment of the new enterprise had to wait until Lyons turned twenty-one years old on 4 September 1922, but the Swallow Sidecar Company was already well on its way.

There were only a handful of employees beside Walmsley and Lyons: a patternmaker, painter, upholsterer and two metalworkers. With so few staff on hand there were long working hours, but the effort was worth it as word spread and more customers were found for the nascent company's products. Moving further afield from the primitive sidecars that Walmsley had first built in his shed, these Swallow Sports models offered various lighting options and chassis that were manufactured by a well-known supplier in Coventry.

In a rather unusual position for such obvious enthusiasts, Walmsley and Lyons eschewed a competition programme, though they supported certain riders on an individual basis. Foreshadowing a policy that would mark the company in the future, the primary focus was on increasing production and profits, rather than the reflected glory that might ensue from winning races. More importantly, the firm was gaining a strong reputation for products that offered outstanding style, packaging and value, hallmarks that would continue through each successive product that appeared over the years.

By 1926, the little company had outgrown its existing space, leading to the purchase of a larger facility, which was made possible by investment from Walmsley's father. With more room, the partners decided to expand their trade offerings to include motorcar repair, body and upholstery work, leading them to adopt a new trade name: The Swallow Sidecar & Coachbuilding Company.

Despite the poor economic conditions prevalent throughout the country, demand for Swallow's sidecars continued to flourish, helped by an association with leading motorcycle manufacturers like Brough Superior. Although pleased with the success of the sidecar line, Lyons was intent to expand into motorcar production, which led him to hire an experienced coachmaker to fabricate the necessary panels. The first car fitted with a Swallow body was a Talbot racecar that had been damaged in an accident, but a more important milestone occurred in January 1927, when the company's agent in Manchester, Stanley Parker, acquired an Austin Seven chassis for Lyons to use as the basis for a new design that was known as the Austin Seven Swallow.

Sidecar production at the Blackpool works in 1930. (Jaguar Land Rover Heritage)

Not long after the company was formed in late 1922, Swallow announced that it was open for business at the works on Cocker Street. (Jaguar Land Rover Heritage)

A flock of Austin Seven Swallows on the production line at Blackpool. (Jaguar Land Rover Heritage)

Despite the steady increase in production at Blackpool, these workers find time to read beside a rack of finished sidecars. (Jaguar Land Rover Heritage)

Introduced in May 1927, it featured an open touring body with distinctive handcrafted aluminium panels that were supported by an ash framework. Despite the minimal dimensions, the car featured an attractive radiator cowl and rounded tail, which lent some flair to the ungainly little roadster. Importantly, Swallow also reinforced the somewhat fragile frame at the rear, improving the underlying automobile as well as making it more attractive. With a list price of only £175, it helped to establish the Swallow brand in the nascent marketplace and paved the way for two larger saloons that followed in 1928.

A pair of significant orders, including one for 500 Austin Swallows, forced the company to increase the scope of its production beyond any previous expectation. With so many new vehicles to build, the company soon relocated in November 1928 to more spacious quarters in Foleshill, just north of Coventry. The move was made with more than a larger facility in mind, since the location allowed the works to draw from a larger pool of skilled labour and put it in a better position to draw from suppliers scattered throughout the West Midlands. By the end of the year, production had increased to almost fifty cars per week, forcing sidecar production into the background. Reflecting the growing reliance on the coachbuilt bodies that had made them so successful, Walmsley and Lyons changed the name of the business to The Swallow Coachbuilding Company, Ltd.

Parting Company

The move to Coventry made possible new models based on Standard, Swift and Fiat chassis, leading to more orders than ever before. Until that time, bespoke coachbuilt bodies were usually reserved for chassis built by more famous and expensive car manufacturers, but Lyons had the touch of the populist, making fashionable style affordable for the masses. Soon, chassis from Morris and Wolseley were added to the mix, finally establishing Swallow as one of the country's premiere coachbuilders, if they were not already considered as such.

Although pleased with the company's success, Lyons wanted to manufacture cars of his own design rather than merely selling 'tarted up' examples of what were otherwise rather prosaic vehicles. He had the good sense to understand that the company could not afford to design its own running gear and chassis, which is how Swallow had got into coachbuilding in the first place, but he wanted more input into the final product than he had in the past.

In 1931, Lyons reached an important agreement with Captain John Black, who ran the Standard Motor Company with a visionary flair. Unlike some manufacturers, Standard was willing to supply components to smaller outfits, unafraid of the potential competition that might result. The terms of the deal included a supply of specially modified chassis based on the Standard Sixteen frame that would be delivered with complete running gear, including rugged and reliable 2,054cc and 2,552cc six-cylinder sidevalve engines.

These components would serve as the foundation for what would become the first proper Swallow model, the SS 1 Coupé, which was introduced at London's

The Austin Seven Swallow Saloon was introduced in October 1928 with bespoke coachwork that made the £187 10s purchase price seem affordable. Due to increased car and sidecar demand, Swallow moved to the Midlands, where most of the company's suppliers were located and there was a broader labour pool. (Jaguar Land Rover Heritage)

The Cocker Street Works in Blackpool. (Jaguar Land Rover Heritage)

Olympia motor show on 9 October 1931. Although not everyone was a fan of the vehicle's appearance, there was no denying that it provided exceptional value for the money at only £310.

Noted for their elegance, affordable price and smooth-running six-cylinder engines, the SS range would eventually grow to encompass several coupés, saloons and an open tourer, later joined by the SS2, a smaller model with four-cylinder power. In 1933 and 1934, the chassis were lengthened and widened to improve their strength and provide better road manners, which also made it possible to introduce a new look for the cars.

Although never having been formally trained as an automotive designer or draftsman, Lyons always had an excellent sense of proportion and beauty, which rarely led him astray when it came to styling. As he was described by Donald Healey:

There is no doubt in my mind that he was the greatest, most inspired, single-handed small motor manufacturer there has ever been or ever will be. His conception of the first SS was truly brilliant, and I maintain that it could never have been achieved by a highly trained, skilled specialist automobile engineer. It had to be done by a man who knew, or sensed, if you like, unerringly what the public wanted, what he himself wanted as a driver, and what would appeal through its individual styling.

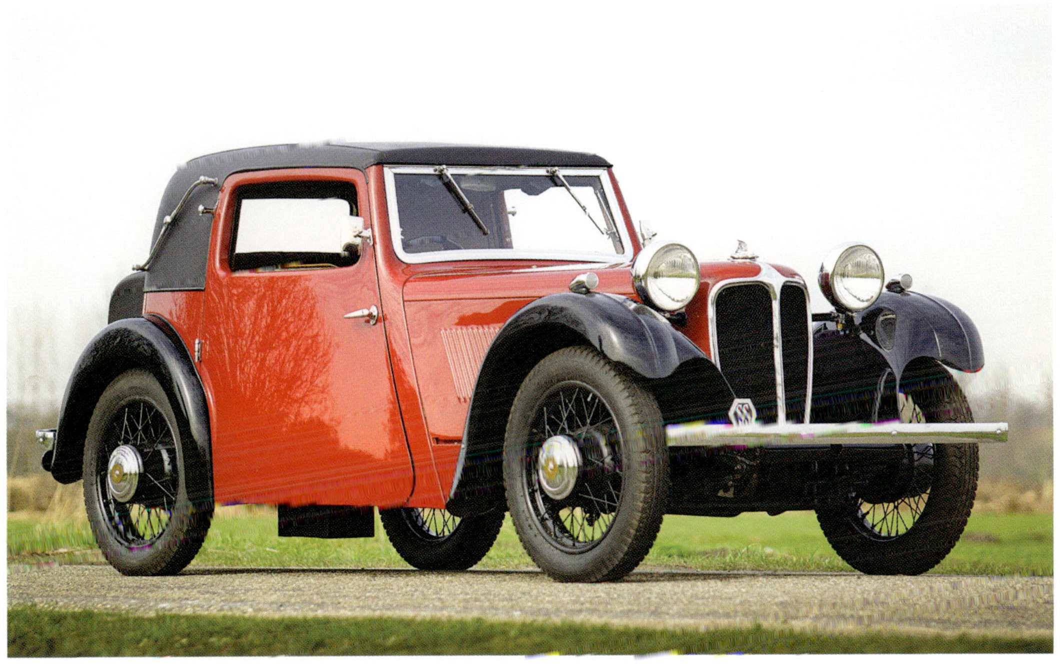

While the SS 1 used the Standard Ensign 16 hp chassis and running gear, the SS 2 was based on the smaller Standard Nippy Nine. This is a 1932 Swallow SS 2 Close Coupled Coupé.

When additional models arrived in 1932, the smaller coupé was restyled in the image of its larger stablemate, though the shorter wheelbase reduced the dramatic effect of the revised coachwork.

Power for the SS 2 came from a Standard 1,052cc sidevalve four-cylinder engine that was mated to a three-speed manual gearbox. In 1934, a larger 1,343cc powerplant was made standard, while a 1,608cc unit was available as an option.

The interior of the SS 2 Coupé was similar to that used in the SS 1, boasting numerous art deco flourishes and extensive wood trim.

A sill plate proclaiming the use of Swallow coachwork. The manufacturer's identification plate was issued by the Standard Motor Company.

This attractive Swallow badge was soon rendered obsolete with the introduction of the Jaguar moniker for the last SS models.

The revised SS 1 introduced the curvaceous Lyons Line that would mark almost every subsequent model through the twenty-first century: the rising fender sweep over the front wheel arches leading to the flowing beltline, before rising again to drape over the rear wheel arches in a delicate transition to the back of the car.

The restyled range offered exceptional value, although the performance was somewhat less than what the athletic styling would suggest. Though not every model met with unabashed consumer enthusiasm, particularly the SS 1 Airline and SS 2, demand was better than expected, which led Lyons to think about adding new models to the range.

With annual production standing at almost 1,800 units, Lyons felt the time was right to hold a public offering to raise money for his plans, but Walmsley was reluctant to entertain further expansion, content with the company's position in the marketplace and unwilling to work harder for an uncertain future.

Throughout 1934, discussions between the two men over the prospect of taking the company public grew heated, leading to Walmsley's departure in early 1935. With his long-time partner gone, Lyons issued stock and established a new entity called SS Cars Limited. The still productive, but much less important, sidecar business was assigned to a subsidiary operating under the old Swallow name, while SS directed its focus toward building cars.

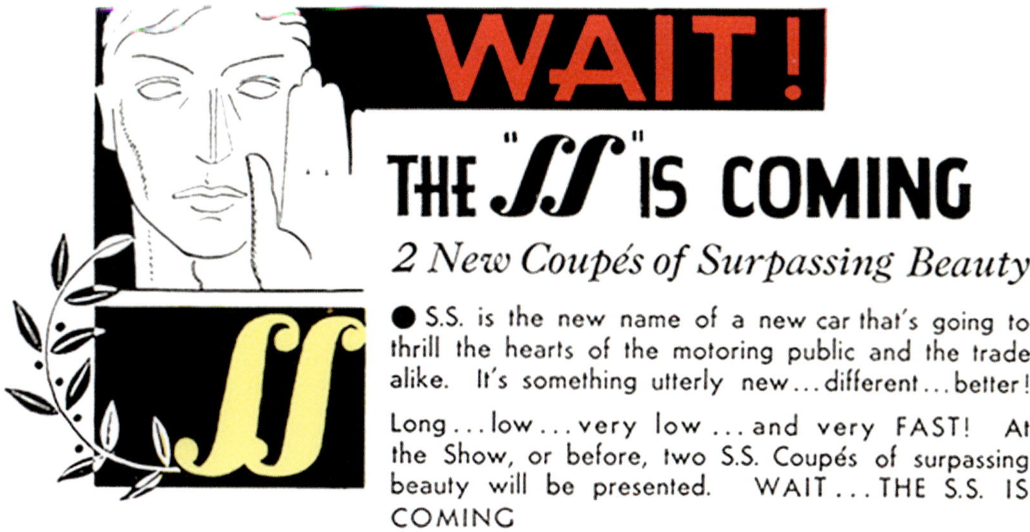

Although the demand for bespoke coachwork allowed Swallow to grow in the midst of the Depression, William Lyons wanted to build a car of his own design. He reached a deal with Captain John Black at Standard for a supply of customised chassis and running gear that would serve as the basis for his SS models, which are hinted at in this 1931 advert. (Jaguar Land Rover Heritage)

Brian Lewis drove this SS 1 Tourer to 55th overall in the 1935 Monte Carlo Rally, which is remembered today for the railway crossing accident that destroyed Triumph's Dolomite Straight Eight with Donald Healey behind the wheel. (Jaguar Land Rover Heritage)

Introduced at the 1931 London Motor Show, William Lyons bestowed the SS 1 with fashionable lines that belied the Standard parts hidden beneath the beautiful coachwork. It was also more affordable than many erstwhile rivals, a trait that would continue well into the future. (Jaguar Land Rover Heritage)

The SS 100 adopted an improved overhead valve cylinder head, in place of the obsolescent sidevalve unit used in its predecessor, to create the first legitimate high-performance model in the SS range. The example shown here was delivered to HRH Prince Michael of Romania. (Jaguar Land Rover Heritage)

16

Aware that the SS 1 and SS 2 offered less performance than their appearance would otherwise suggest, Lyons was keen to improve matters by introducing a true sports car that would do real justice to his styling ability. Launched in March 1935, the SS 90 was built on a shortened version of the SS 1 chassis that was fitted with contemporary flowing roadster coachwork. Powered by the Standard 2,663cc engine used in the SS 1, it offered a 90 mph top speed and good handling but even better things were in the offing that would finally address the performance question satisfactorily.

Throughout the previous year, Lyons had been consumed with extracting more power from the Standard engine which, he thought, 'Just couldn't pull the skin off a rice pudding!' Harry Weslake, the finest cylinder head specialist of the era, had been retained to help solve the problem, which led him to design a new overhead valve cylinder head that helped to push the output from 75 bhp to 104 bhp at 4,500 rpm with a hotter camshaft and dual carburettors.

This improved power plant continued to be manufactured by Standard and was soon ready in sufficient quantities for the company to introduce a whole new range before the end of the year. Bringing three models to market in such a short period of time was an impossible task, but it was accomplished with the help of William Heynes, whom Lyons had hired as Chief Engineer on the recommendation of several industry contacts.

In September 1935, the SS 100 sports car and 1-½ and 2-½ Litre Saloons were introduced at the May Fair Hotel to an enthusiastic reception from the company's sales agents and the assembled press. Along with their immediate predecessors, these models placed SS on a whole new tier in the marketplace.

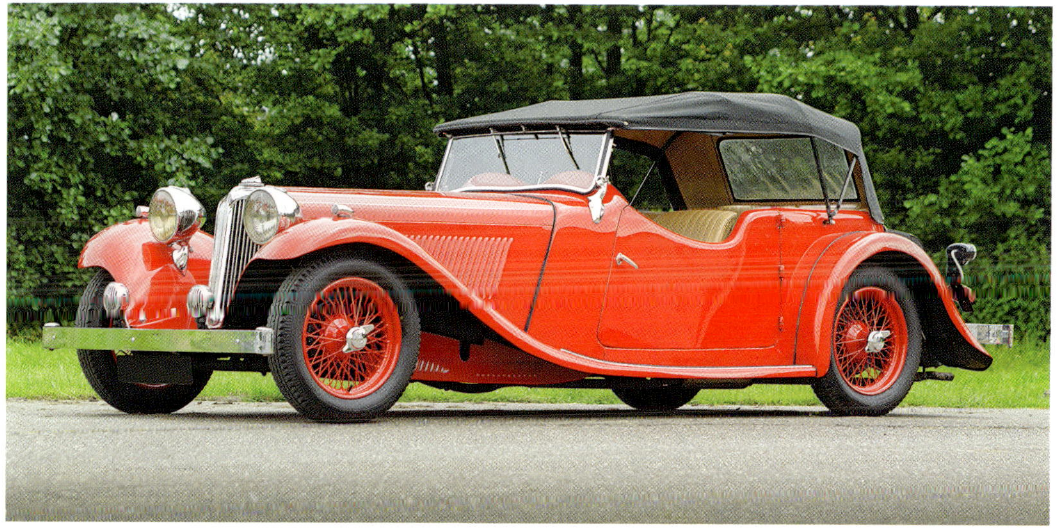

The SS 1 Tourer was produced from 1933 to 1936. It was built in both 16 and 20 hp versions with an initial starting price of £325. A number of striking colour schemes were available. This restored example was built in 1934.

The sculptured deep armchair seats seen in this SS 1 Tourer were emblematic of the breed prior to the introduction of the SS-Jaguar models.

The SS 1 Coupé was the spiritual forerunner to the Jaguars that followed after the war, boasting appealing styling, attractive features and an affordable price. Built upon a Standard Ensign underslung chassis that had been specially modified according to Lyons's instructions, a wider track of 4 feet 5 inches appeared in 1934.

A new body style for the SS 1 appeared in 1933, establishing a treasured visual identity for the company. Lyons would revisit the long bonnet proportions used here for all of the sporting models designed under his watch. Even the twenty-first-century F-Type relies on this basic layout.

Power for the SS 1 came from the Standard 2.1/2.6-litre engine. By the time that this 1934 example was manufactured, an improved cylinder head, more efficient manifolds and a slight displacement increase to 2,143cc and 2,663cc raised the top speed to 75 mph.

Most of the SS models from this era featured flamboyant upholstery inspired by the contemporary art deco movement. The sunburst motif seen on the door panels appeared in a number of models.

The Nazi Schutzstaffel made continued use of the SS moniker impractical after the war, more so due to the similarity between this badge and the insignia adopted by the hated paramilitary organisation.

Rather than customers viewing the firm as mere coachbuilders, SS was now seen as a proper manufacturer, even if it still relied mainly on components sourced from Standard. What was important is that they were able to prove that the sum was greater than the parts involved, especially when they could improve them as Weslake had shown with his innovative overhead valve cylinder head.

Only twenty-three examples of the SS 90 were built in 1935. Power came from the Standard 20 sidevalve 2,633cc engine that produced 68 bhp. Built upon a shortened version of the SS 1 chassis, both the styling and handling were at the head of the class but the performance was mediocre at best. That shortcoming was rectified with the SS 100 and its overhead valve power plant.

For the SS 100 and 2-½ Litre Saloons, the over the road performance finally proved a match for the sensuous styling. Some of the best-handling automobiles of their era, both models exhibited pleasant road manners to go along with strong acceleration and a reservoir of torque that made pulling up hills a pleasure. As described in *The Motor,* 'With a distinguished appearance, outstanding performance and attractive price as the main characteristics, the new SS Jaguar range represents an achievement of which Mr Lyons and his technical staff may well feel proud.'

These cars also introduced the Jaguar name to the world. As many have asserted over the years, several Brough motorcycles likely inspired the SS moniker, though Lyons himself asserted that the initials had no specific meaning. For the vastly improved models that were on the horizon, Lyons wanted something to distinguish them from their immediate predecessors. After considering a variety of animal, fish and bird names, he settled on Jaguar, influenced by his emotional attachment to an Armstrong Siddeley airplane engine of the same name.

The SS Jaguars, particularly the saloons, cemented the company's reputation as a purveyor of exceptional motorcars at an affordable price. Over the next few years, Lyons introduced changes to increase performance rather than profitability. In that vein, all-steel construction arrived and more efficient production methods were introduced, which led sales past the 14,000-unit level and brought a small profit in 1938. Although the firm's further growth would be put on hold with the onset of the Second World War, Lyons and company would use the time wisely, building armaments that would help save the nation and designing an engine that would power a legend.

Chapter 2
Head of the Class

By the time that hostilities erupted in September 1939, most British factories were consumed with rearmament and throughout the conflict both SS and Swallow produced war materiel, including aircraft parts for the Spitfire and Mosquito fighters and the Lancaster and Stirling heavy bombers. During the Battle of Britain, sporadic Luftwaffe attacks struck at the important manufacturing facilities scattered across the West Midlands, causing little damage but fraying nerves and interrupting production. These nuisance strikes, however, served as a prelude to more air raids, which culminated in a massive bombing mission on the night of 14 November 1940 that destroyed or damaged many of Coventry's industrial structures and caused almost 2,000 civilian casualties.

Air raids continued on a limited basis throughout 1942 but as the war progressed the primary threat came from unmanned V-1 flying bombs and V-2 rockets that were fired from hidden locations in northern France and the Netherlands. Although these strikes were mainly directed at London and the South East, Coventrians were forced to work under strict blackout conditions that required each business to maintain a nightly fire watch. Never one to delegate unpleasant tasks, Lyons did his duty once a week, serving as a lookout from a small room inside the Foleshill works.

With the tide of the war having turned during 1943, standing fire watch became rather tedious since few attacks occurred to break the boredom. Showing the foresight that marked his career, Lyons assembled a small team of his most trusted employees to stand watch with him on Sunday nights, consisting of William Heynes, Claude Baily and Walter Hassan. Once assembled, Lyons would discuss planning and design issues, devising a strategy for what to do once peace arrived.

Although lacking a formal engineering education, Lyons had an obvious affinity for the work and possessed a brilliant understanding of what customers wanted, being able to predict market trends with an amazing precision. He had spent much of the war modelling prospective styling treatments, using his inimitable design ethos to fashion shapes that could remain contemporary long into the future.

While many topics were discussed by the quartet during these Sunday strategy sessions, much of the debate centred around future engine requirements, especially since all four engineers agreed that it was best to move away from the Standard power plants that had been used for the company's pre-war models. Lyons wanted to design and build an entire family of engines in both four and six-cylinder form, engines that were more advanced, more refined and far more powerful than the Standard units.

The Jaguar workforce shifted their focus to munitions production throughout the Second World War, including building fuselage and wing sections for the Gloster Meteor, which would serve as Britain's first jet fighter. (Jaguar Land Rover Heritage)

William Heynes CBE inspects an engine during his Jaguar tenure. Although he joined the company as a chassis engineer, he played an instrumental role in the design and development of the legendary XK engine. (Graham Robson Collection)

The parameters for the proposed power plant were simple: it had to feature an advanced design that would obviate the need for constant upgrades, offer exceptional performance with an output around 160 bhp, be simple and inexpensive to build and possess a distinctive visual appeal that reflected the quality of the internal parts, while looking 'smart and powerful' at the same time.

What transpired from the small office in Foleshill became the second-most powerful engine in the world, behind only Cadillac's massive V-8, and was the first mass-produced power plant to feature dual overhead camshafts and an alloy cylinder head with hemispherical combustion chambers. More importantly, it became an engineering icon and changed the course of the company forever.

As the war reached its waning stages in Europe, Lyons formed Jaguar Cars on 23 March 1945, having recognised that the Third Reich had permanently debauched any remaining commercial value in the SS moniker. A number of other animal names were considered at the time but the familiarity with the feline moniker from the pre-war models was too strong an advantage for the other candidates to overcome. Intent on concentrating his resources and attention on automobile production, Lyons sold off the sidecar business in January 1946 to the Helliwell Group. With no other distractions, Lyons focused on getting the works back into the habit of building cars after the long hiatus made necessary by the war; there was much to be done.

Although the first cars built during those early days after the war were the same as those that had been produced in the late 1930s, Lyons appreciated that his company could not long rely on antebellum models once the rest of the industry got back on its feet. Because saloons, rather than sports cars, generated the most profits, Lyons ordered that maximum effort go towards preparing a modern design that could reach the market as soon as possible.

One of the most significant hurdles to overcome was obtaining an adequate supply of steel, rubber and other goods to make volume production of a new car commercially viable. The new Labour government was strictly rationing raw materials, reserving them for companies that could earn hard currency on the export market to rebuild the troubled economy, which forced Jaguar to meet with the Ministry of Supply for a permit to procure the necessary supplies.

After several meetings, Jaguar received the authorisation for materials that it required, but the saloon project ran into unforeseen difficulties that threatened its proposed launch, scheduled for late 1948. Faced with the prospect of a delayed introduction for the important flagship saloon, Lyons ordered a crash program to prepare a sports car to display at the London Motor Show in October. Lyons wanted something that could create a stir, showcasing both the XK engine and the new chassis that had been developed for the saloon models. It could also test these untried components under real world conditions, while garnering valuable press for the marque, just as the Mk VII should be reaching the market.

King of the Jungle

The new sports car was built around the XK power plant that had been laid out during the war. Originally, four different versions of the basic design had been built to test them in operation, code named XF, XG, XJ-4 and XJ-6. Except for the XG, each variant was fitted with dual overhead camshafts and the hemispherical crossflow cylinder head that Weslake had championed for performance reasons. The most promising candidate among the four was the XJ-6, displacing 3,181cc and producing 147 bhp at 5,000 rpm.

Although the power output was acceptable, it lacked sufficient torque, which was remedied by lengthening the stroke to 106 mm, resulting in an engine with a total displacement of 3,442cc. As modified, it produced 160 bhp at 5,400 rpm and 195 pound-feet of torque at only 2,500 rpm, offering better than expected performance and smooth operation.

Because the camshafts were located in the cylinder head, the webbed cast iron engine block was strong but light. It housed a forged EN16 manganese molybdenum steel counterbalanced crankshaft that turned in seven main bearings with connecting rods fashioned from the same material. Aluminium pistons reduced reciprocating mass and ran in unlined cylinder bores, while the Weslake cylinder head was made with DTD424 alloy, saving half the weight from a similar cast iron unit. The twin camshafts ran in four bearings and were driven by Duplex roller chains, acting directly on the inclined valves.

Until the overwhelming clamour surrounding the XK120's appearance at Earls Court, Jaguar had intended to build only 200 examples clad with aluminium body panels. The delay in tooling up for volume production meant that relatively few vehicles reached customers before May 1950, when the first steel-bodied versions arrived. Note the vents to cool the brakes located under the front bumpers.

Particularly when fitted with spatted rear wheels, the XK120 OTS bears a strong resemblance to the 1938 BMW Mille Miglia Bügelfalte. Most examples fitted with disc wheels were equipped with spats for the rear wheels.

Note the ventilator in the front wing that appeared in February 1951 to address customer complaints regarding excessive cabin heat. Equipped with a mesh screen to prevent debris from entering the cabin, it allowed fresh air into the footwells. (John Goodman)

The alloy and early steel-bodied cars shared an identical dashboard layout, designed to facilitate both left and right-hand steering. The tachometer was always placed closest to the driver, while the speedometer was located nearest the passenger.

There are numerous interior detail differences between the alloy and steel versions, as well as some subtle alterations made during the production run. This 1951 example features the heavily contoured seatback that identified the early cars.

The door pocket changed position between the early and later examples, while the door strap shown here arrived in September 1949.

North American examples were typically fitted with sealed beam headlamps, but all others were usually equipped with the Lucas PF.770 tripod units shown here. Note that the housing for the side lamp is faired into the wing. Until September 1952 they were contained in a separate chromed housing.

One of the most successful and longest serving engines ever built, Jaguar's XK unit endured from 1947 to 1992 in various forms. Incorporating the best quality internal components that were available at the time and an advanced design that produced generous torque and good horsepower, it powered everything from the Le Mans-winning sports racers to several luxury saloons, not to mention several armoured vehicles.

The XK engine as fitted to the XK120 could be ordered with three different compression ratios: 7:1 for export models, 8:1 for the home market and 9:1 at the customer's special request. The first specification resulted in 150 bhp at 5,400 rpm, while the second produced 160 bhp at the same engine speed. The SE versions were more powerful, producing 180 bhp at 5,750 rpm with the 8:1 compression pistons. Later cars had the ignition coil relocated above the forward carburettor. SU H6 carburettors with shorter dashpots were introduced in April 1950.

Four distinct Moss gearbox variants – SH, JH, JL and SL – were fitted to the XK120. The later JL and SL versions appeared in February 1952 and featured a revised housing with a shorter main shaft than the earlier types. An optional close-ratio gearbox was available for special orders.

The alloy cars had a more fully trimmed boot than this early steel-bodied example. A Hardura mat replaced the carpeting shown here in November 1952. The tool roll seen to the left of the tyre is typical of those supplied to most XK120s and the earliest XK140s.

The iconic Bugatti Type 57C Atalante probably inspired the shape of the XK120 FHC's roof, which also appeared in similar form on a specially constructed SS 100 Coupé displayed at the 1938 London Motor Show. Note the similarities between the backlights used for the XK120 FHC and Mark VII saloon, save for the lack of surrounding bright trim on the sports car.

To ensure reliability and longevity, almost every internal component was constructed from the best materials available: chilled cast iron tappet guides, silicon-chromed steel intake and austenitic steel exhaust valves, not to mention the crankshaft, connecting rods and pistons discussed above.

A low-pressure lubrication system was designed to reduce drag and increase pumping efficiency. The twin-branch exhaust manifolds were coated with vitreous enamel and led to dual pipes that exited as a single piece at the back. Dual SU H6 1¾-inch carburettors, fed by an electric fuel pump, were mounted on a cast aluminium intake manifold, which featured an integrated water jacket to provide more consistent operational temperatures.

The Moss gearbox was sourced from the contemporary saloons, featuring four speeds with no synchromesh on first gear, driven through a single plate 10-inch Borg & Beck clutch. Power was transmitted through a Hardy Spicer propeller shaft and an ENV rear axle, which was later replaced by a similar unit from Salisbury. Lockheed four-wheel drum brakes with twin leading shoes up front were operated from a single chassis-mounted master cylinder, marking the company's first use of hydraulics.

For use in a smaller sports car, a Mk V chassis was shortened and narrowed under Bob Knight's supervision, resulting in a 102-inch wheelbase and 51-inch front and 50-inch rear tracks. Because it had started out as the basis for a saloon, the final product was extraordinarily robust, featuring box section side members and two crossmembers located at the front and middle, supplemented by a lighter box section over the rear axle that supported the rear bodywork and mounted the rear springs. The bodywork's bulk was supported by four outriggers, which were located to either side of the centre crossmember, mounted just forward of where the frame rose sharply to provide increased suspension movement over the rear axle.

Heynes and Knight developed the independent front suspension based on the former's previous work before the war, which had been inspired by the Citroën Traction Avant. It featured an upper and lower wishbone layout with longitudinal manganese torsion bars mounted to adjusters on the centre chassis crossmember. A Newton telescopic shock absorber was attached to the lower wishbones, mounted at an angle on a bracket positioned above and inboard of the upper wishbone. The stub axle carriers were positioned with ball joints, while the lower suspension beams were linked with an antiroll bar that was mounted in rubber. Burman recirculating ball steering gear was located in a trunnion on the upper wishbone bracket, attached to a long column oriented at a 10 degree incline from the horizontal and a massive Bluemel four-spoke steering wheel. The rear suspension was traditional in the extreme, featuring Girling PV7 frame-mounted lever-arm dampers and conventional semi-elliptical leaf springs.

An artist rendering of the XK120 prepared for the model's introductory brochure. (British Sports Car Hall of Fame)

Charles H. Hornburg Jr, Jaguar's distributor on the United States West Coast, and Arthur Rippey, an advertising executive from Denver, admire the sleek lines of the XK120 prototype at Earls Court in October 1948. (Jaguar Land Rover Heritage)

Although clearly derivative of several previous designs, particularly the BMW 328, Lyons created a lithesome shape that was the perfect match to the potent performance provided by the XK engine. Blessed with the same Lyons Line that had marked the SS 100, the body combined powerful curves with smooth sides, producing a memorable shape that would inspire numerous imitators such as the Daimler Conquest, Jowett Jupiter and Triumph TR2. Remarkably, the iconic styling effort took less than two weeks to complete, with Lyons personally directing the activity of metalworkers and fitters to achieve the physical form that he had envisioned in his mind's eye.

Since the sports car had been intended to serve as a glamour project and technical showcase for the advanced XK engine, it was designed from the start with limited production in mind, using alloy panels formed over a laminated ash internal framework, with steel used only for the chassis frame, inner structure and forward bulkhead. The long alligator bonnet was a dominant styling feature, displaying a sharp triangular shape when viewed from above and a beautifully integrated oval radiator grille. The bonnet was set between flowing front wings with broad flanks that swept down toward the cutaway doors, while powerful haunches formed over the rear wheels before tapering off to a smooth tail.

By Popular Demand

Introduced in October 1948 at the London Motor Show at Earls Court, the XK120 Super Sports Open Two Seater met with rapturous enthusiasm from both press and public. Although there were countless reasons for the infatuation, including the beautiful styling and the promise of potent performance, most attractive to potential customers was the £998 list price, which undercut anything comparable by a healthy margin. Within a week it was clear that the initial plans for only limited production would have to be abandoned, since there were already hundreds of orders on the books for the impressive new car. Before the doors had closed on the show, Lyons had made arrangements with Pressed Steel to start work on manufacturing production body panels from steel. Even with this head start, the first 240 examples were built with alloy coachwork as the company tried to turn what had they had thought would be a limited quantity hand-built sports car into a best-seller for the masses.

To prove that the 120 stood for an actual performance figure rather than a number plucked from the air, Lyons sent an XK120 to the Jabbeke Highway for a high-speed test before a number of motoring journalists and officials from the Royal Automobile Club of Belgium. With Lyons and Heynes watching with intense interest, Ron 'Soapy' Sutton took the wheel, a last-minute replacement for Walter Hassan, who had fallen ill.

132·6 M.P.H. ON PUMP PETROL · · ·

The XK120 caused a sensation with its unexpected appearance at the 1948 London Motor Show, but even more impressive was the performance on tap from the XK engine, which made it the fastest production car in the world. (British Sports Car Hall of Fame)

On 30 May 1949, Ron 'Soapy' Sutton piloted an XK120 fitted with an aluminium undertray, tonneau cover, metal windscreen and rear-wheel spats to 132.596 mph on the Jabbeke Highway in Belgium, making it the fastest production car in the world. Originally, Walter Hassan was to have driven, but an illness forced his replacement by the diminutive test driver. (Jaguar Land Rover Heritage)

With standard running gear under the skin, but fitted with an aluminium undertray, a small metal windscreen and a full-length tonneau cover to improve the aerodynamics, the XK120 managed an astounding 132.596 mph, setting the record for the fastest production car in the world.

It was a signal accomplishment that received significant attention in the press, which pushed demand to even more dizzying heights, but it took time to transition from the first hand-assembled cars to their mass-production counterparts. The first steel-bodied versions did not appear until April 1950, featuring several changes from the alloy cars, including slight differences in the external body panels and introduction of all-steel construction for the sills and door shut faces. Aluminium continued to be used for the bonnet, door skins and boot lid, however, but changes were made to various other components, including the door hinges and the shape of the internal bulkheads.

In its first test of an XK120, *Road & Track* recorded a 123.2 mph maximum speed and acceleration from 0 to 60 mph in 10.1 seconds, better numbers than *The Autocar* had recorded. More impressive was the subjective evaluation that the car received from the editors, who wrote that 'driving the Jaguar XK-120 is an experience not soon forgotten'.

A publicity still depicting an XK120 OTS and FHC, taken at an event to promote the Mark VII saloon's introduction in late 1951. (Graham Robson Collection)

Film icon Clark Gable took delivery of the first XK120 officially sold in the United States and became an enthusiastic marque advocate. In March 1950 he penned an article for *Road & Track*, writing, 'The car is the easiest handling vehicle I have maneuvered at any speed or condition.' He later owned a second example that was modified at the factory for improved cabin ventilation, engine cooling and luggage capacity. (Jaguar Land Rover Heritage)

The Jaguar XKSS was a thinly disguised version of the D-type sports racer, built by converting twenty-five complete and partially finished examples into road-going trim with a number of simple modifications, including a door for the passenger, better weather protection, full windscreen, comprehensive lighting and vestigial bumpers. The sixteen examples that survived the Browns Lane fire are among the most valuable cars in the world with a projected worth of £12–15 million. (Jaguar Land Rover Heritage)

Few publications found any real fault with the car, aside from the minor ergonomic quibbles that were part and parcel of most sports car designs, though there were real shortcomings that went unmentioned, including excessive cabin heat and brakes that were prone to fade with repeated use. With so much time and effort devoted to satisfying demand, few running modifications were made during the early production run, other than a more efficient radiator, shorter carburettor dashpots and a smaller oil sump, which all arrived in 1950.

A more momentous change occurred in March 1951, when Jaguar introduced the fixed-head coupé at the International Motor Show in Geneva. A sportier companion to the distinguished Mk VII, it offered similar levels of comfort and luxury as the saloon but retained the potent performance for which the XK120 was famous. The attractive steel roof mimicked the shape pioneered in the Bugatti Type 57 Aérolithe, Atalante and Atlantic coupés, but it also boasted similarities with a pre-war coupé version of the SS 100 that had been displayed at Olympia before the war.

In closed form, the austere roadster was transformed into a preeminent grand touring car that offered niceties such as a heater, lockable glove compartment, external door handles and locks, rollup windows, opening quarter lights, tinted sun visors, footwell ventilation, courtesy lamps and an opulent interior featuring walnut veneer trim on the dashboard, door caps and side window surrounds, as well as a wool headliner.

The mohair hood, as depicted in this photograph, was revised in February 1951 with a longer rear and a zippered backlight surround. The hood itself was unlined and secured to the header rail with three toggle clamps.

This commemorative plate was used to pay tribute to Ron Sutton's record run at Jabbeke in 1949. It was fitted to cars sold with an 8:1 compression ratio in certain markets, including Belgium, Canada, Norway, Sweden, Switzerland and the United States. A similar plate celebrating the later Jabbeke record appeared in 1953 for OTS SE models. The more powerful engines in these cars featured uprated camshafts and valve springs, shorter valve and tappet guides, a lightened flywheel and a special crankshaft damper. These special models were also fitted with a Burgess dual exhaust system, stiffer torsion bars and stronger rear springs.

Introduced in March 1951, the XK120 FHC bodyshell displayed numerous minor differences from the open version, including alterations to the front wing design and A-pillar. Unlike the wooden floors used in the OTS, the closed cars had steel replacements that had a small plywood section fitted in the heel area. American dealers commonly fitted whitewall tyres, as shown here. (John Goodman)

Although the XK120 FHC boasted a similar cabin layout to the OTS, the furnishings were far more luxurious with a walnut fascia and door trim, not to mention the advantage of rollup windows.

The XK120's rear overriders provided minimal protection during parking shunts, which Jaguar addressed by fitting robust rear quarter bumpers for the XK140. The rear lamps were set in small alloy housings that were finished in chrome plating.

Introduced in April 1953, the XK120 DHC combined elements from both its open and closed siblings, allowing the fortunate owner to choose between open motoring and enclosed comfort depending on whim and weather. The aluminium skins for the doors were replaced with steel in December 1953, although the frame itself was still constructed largely with wood.

Unlike the unlined unit fitted to the OTS, the mohair hood on the DHC boasted multi-layer construction and a more complex frame arrangement. As with the hood fitted to the later open cars, the backlight could be opened with a zipper for better ventilation. Note the chrome trim strips that helped create a more luxurious image for the model.

The DHC offered the same sumptuous cabin appointments and instrument layout as the FHC, but with some minor differences and additional interior lighting. When fitted, the radio occupied the space where the drawer is located at the lower part of the fascia.

The XK120 offered a distinctive profile from the OTS and FHC. Due to the more complex hood and window arrangement, there were numerous changes made to the basic body structure, including the integrated windscreen frame, fuller doors, relocated fuel filler and a shorter centre tonneau section.

40

Despite the thicker doors that were made necessary with the appearance of rollup windows, there was more interior room and increased storage with a sliding drawer, parcel shelf and concealed locker that could hold a plethora of small items and papers. In addition to the luxurious kit, these cars also marked the introduction of self-adjusting front brakes, fender vents, and the wider availability of fifty-four-spoke, 16-inch wire wheels that were available on both models, while the heater was made optional on the roadster.

Predictably, the coupé was warmly greeted by the press and public alike as the most affordable, accessible, and reliable grand touring coupé on the market, making it an attractive alternative to more exclusive models like the Alfa Romeo 6C, Aston Martin DB2, Bristol 401 and Talbot-Lago T26 Grand Sport. Combining sports car performance with hitherto unknown levels of comfort, it proved popular with customers that wanted an automobile that was more practical than the open roadster.

To take advantage of the C-type's victory at the 1951 24 Hours of Le Mans, the company published a special pamphlet entitled *Tuning Modification on XK120 Cars for Competition Purposes*, detailing the equipment and procedures required to extract maximum performance for competition and fast road use. It was also possible to order the special components discussed in the book as a factory package, resulting in the XK120 SE, which was called the 'M' in North America.

The assembly line at Browns Lane in the early 1950s, featuring a number of Mark VII saloons and XK120s. (Jaguar Land Rover Heritage)

The new model featured an uprated clutch, higher lift camshafts, performance distributor and spark plugs, lightened flywheel, 8:1 compression pistons, a special crankshaft damper, custom carburettor needles, heavy-duty leaf springs and a dual exhaust. For an additional fee, it was also possible to add thicker torsion bars, heavier duty springs, more radical camshafts and higher compression pistons. Fitted with these modifications, the SE became a street legal racing car, producing 180 bhp, or 190 bhp with the optional 9:1 pistons and uprated camshafts, which made it possible to reach 60 mph from a stop in only 8.5 seconds.

In 1952, production shifted from Foleshill to Browns Lane. Although the new facility was located only 2 miles away, it took almost the entire year to complete the move. With so much effort devoted to the transition, it was a quiet year for running improvements, which were limited to revised side lamps, an improved fuel gauge, new switchgear, windscreen washers, wider road wheels and demister vents for the roadster. The stiffer springs from the SE were adopted as standard equipment on both open and closed models, while metallic paint was eliminated as an option.

The best traits of the XK120 coupé and roadster were combined when the drophead coupé appeared at the New York Motor Show in March 1953. Unlike the primitive top that provided little more than basic weather protection for the open two-seater, the drophead coupé offered an excellent convertible top, which featured an external mohair layer with bonded canvas insulation and a fabric headliner. The rear window could be unzipped to improve ventilation and the entire assembly could be operated from a seated position in mere seconds. When erected, it provided the same quietude and refinement as the coupé and featured that model's wood trim, larger doors and front quarter lights, but with frameless side windows to preserve the pleasant lines when the glass was lowered.

On sale for less than two years, the drophead was produced in the fewest numbers of the XK120 range and featured in only one major road test, which was published in *Autosport*. As expected, the review was positive, with John Bolster writing: 'A long run in this car is a pleasure that is difficult to put into words. Whether it is its complete indifference to all kinds of road surface, its silence and smoothness, or the feeling of always having more power in reserve, I know not.'

The XK120's crown as the world's fastest sports car fell to a Pegaso Z-102 in September 1953, leading Lyons to instruct Norman Dewis, the company's chief test engineer, to make immediate plans to snatch it back. Although short of stature, Dewis was a giant in terms of intellect and drive, allowing him to prepare a worthy contender for the throne in only a few weeks.

Unlike the car that Sutton had driven in 1949, which appeared not much different from a standard example, Dewis created an aerodynamic wonder, with a metal tonneau cover, streamlined headlamps and a bubble canopy that looked as if it had been plucked straight from a Hawker Sea Fury. Where the Spanish sports car had managed 151.042 mph, Dewis demolished the month-old record with an amazing 172.412 mph run, making the XK120 the fastest production car in the world once again.

The XK120 remained the world's fastest production car until late 1953, when a Pegaso Z-102 reached 151.042 mph over the flying kilometre. Unhappy with this development, Sir William Lyons instructed Norman Dewis to prepare an XK120 to retake the record. Here, Dewis is pictured with his modified car in front of a control station operated by the Belgian Royal Automobile Club. (Jaguar Land Rover Heritage)

Unlike Sutton's relatively standard example, XK120 MDU 254 featured a number of performance enhancements, including an increased compression ratio for the XK engine and a close-ration gearbox, but the most visible changes were comprehensive aerodynamic modifications that included a bubble canopy, smaller headlight fairings and narrow tyres filled to 50 psi. Barely a month after Pegaso had taken the crown from the XK120, Dewis recorded an astounding 172.412 mph over the same stretch of Belgian highway to take it back. (Jaguar Land Rover Heritage)

Over the remaining eighteen months of production, the XK120 continued to sell well, propelled to new heights by the introduction of the drophead in 1953 and the publicity from the latest achievement in Belgium. With such strong demand and few inherent vices, substantive changes were few, mostly relating to revised instrumentation, construction materials and varying wheel packages, but larger 2-inch carburettors became an option in 1954.

By the time that production for the XK120 ended later that summer, Jaguar had produced 12,059 XK120s, comprised of 7,614 roadsters, 2,678 fixed-head coupés and 1,767 drophead coupés. Not surprisingly, the overwhelming majority were sold in the United States, which took delivery of 9,096 examples. As one of the sports car pioneers in that important export market, Jaguar eventually found itself a target for a host of new competitors such as Mercedes-Benz and Porsche, which forced it to introduce improvements to their flagship sports car to keep it on top in terms of performance and consumer demand.

Lyons contemplated replacement of the XK120 with a striking modern design and may have done so if the resources had been available. With strong demand for the Mk VII and a smaller saloon entering the final stages of development, there was simply not enough capacity to tool up production for a completely new design, much less one that was sold in fewer numbers than the more popular family cars. Weighing these factors, Jaguar faced the pragmatic truth, ensuring that the next XK represented a difference in degree rather than in kind.

Although special bodies were primarily reserved for Continental models, a few XKs received this attention, including memorable examples from designers including Abbott, Bertone, Boano and Zagato. This 1954 XK120 SE debuted at the 1955 Geneva Auto Salon bearing distinctive Pinin Farina coachwork. It was built for Max Hoffman, who was instrumental in the success of the sports car movement in the US through his influential New York-based dealership. (Jaguar Land Rover Heritage)

Chapter 3
A Better Breed of Cat

Replacing an icon is never simple, but Jaguar focused on incremental refinements and improved creature comforts when it introduced the XK140 at Earls Court in 1954. Despite retaining the same basic bodyshell as the XK120, the new model appeared far more substantial, though the few changes that were made subtracted from the exceptional purity of the original design, making it less likely to tug on the emotions or stir passions within the soul.

By almost any objective measure, however, the XK140 was the superior automobile, offering more interior space, higher performance and better road manners than the car it replaced, factors that were becoming more important to customers who were less accepting of the crude sports cars that had dominated the market in the first few years after the war.

During those halcyon days, models like the XK120 and MG TC were what enthusiasts imagined when asked to describe the perfect automobile, but throughout the 1950s more sybaritic pleasures became more important, such as rollup windows, proper weather equipment and comfortable cabins. Although both coupé variants of the XK120 line addressed all those concerns to some degree, there were still ergonomic shortcomings that could be improved on, winning further converts for the marque.

Produced in the same three variants as the XK120 – open two-seater, fixed-head coupé and drophead coupé – there was a renewed emphasis on practicality and comfort throughout

Manufactured between 1954 and 1957, the XK140 was a greatly improved vehicle offering more interior room, better brakes, a more compliant suspension and rack and pinion steering. (Jaguar Land Rover Heritage)

the XK140 range. Although the heavy bumpers with their robust overriders added unwanted weight, increased overall length and cluttered the styling, they were far more useful than the dainty chromed bits that had adorned the XK120, especially in America, where parking by feel was an unfortunate national pastime.

Given the rushed gestation of the XK120, there were a number of features that made their way into production that were more suited to a bespoke hand-built sports car than the mass-produced darling that it became after the euphoric reception that greeted it at Earls Court. With such strong sales figures, some of these expensive accoutrements would have to give way to less expensive substitutes in a nod to the accountants. One such example was the XK120 grille, featuring chrome-on-brass construction and assembled with an appealing array of delicate slats. For the XK140, a cruder cast substitute appeared with fewer slats but incorporating an enamel badge to replace the iconic growler emblem that had been proudly attached to the XK120's bonnet. At least some of the savings went to pay for other additions, some more worthwhile than others, such as more shiny bits to woo the American market. These included bolder headlamp rims, larger plinths for the rear lights and trim strips that ran down the centre of the bonnet and boot lid, which were, thank goodness, still fashioned from aluminium.

This photograph shows the revised cast zinc alloy grille, bonnet finishing strip, integral indicator lamps and stouter bumper assembly that visually distinguish the front of the XK140 from its predecessor. Although hidden by the bumper assembly, the brake cooling vents were enlarged and made a different shape to increase efficiency.

The XK140 boot lid featured a chrome trim strip and a prominent badge touting the marque's success at the 24 Hours of Le Mans.

This XK140 OTS is finished in the rare original livery of lavender grey over biscuit. It was originally delivered to Los Angeles, California, in March 1955.

The XK140 OTS used essentially the same side curtains as the previous model with a steel frame and mohair fabric. The flap seen at the bottom is to allow for the use of hand signals. A satchel made from Rexine cloth protected the side curtains during storage.

The XK140 introduced a repositioned engine, moved forward by 3 inches to increase cabin room. The forward bulkhead was also relocated to suit and raised by an additional inch, while the footwells projected farther into the engine compartment than before.

The badge on the valve cover identifies an engine fitted with the optional C-type cylinder head. In this form the XK engine produced 210 bhp at 5,750 rpm and 213 pound-feet of torque at 4,000 rpm.

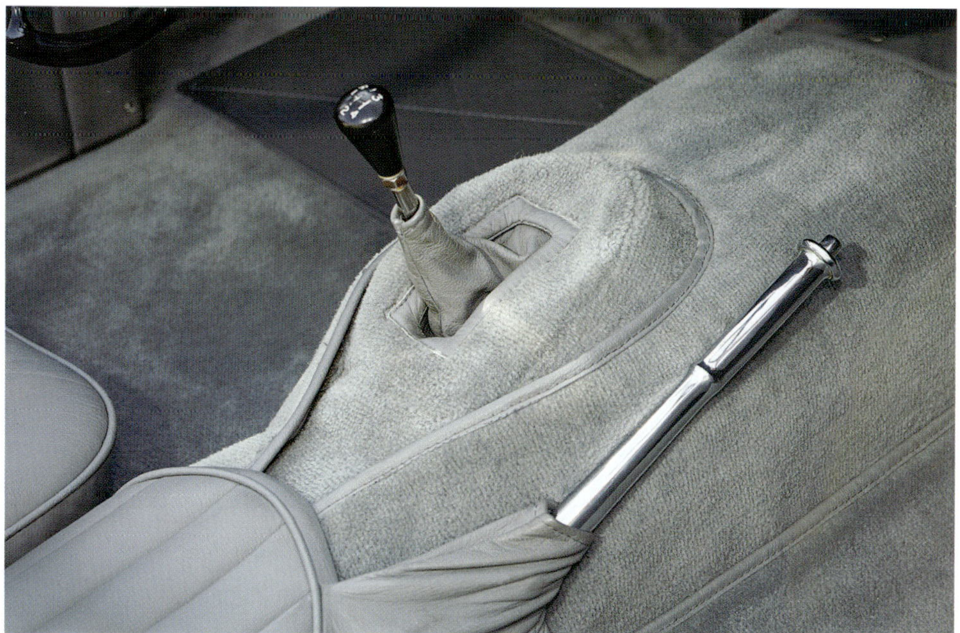

The XK140 used the same Moss JL and SL short main-shaft gearbox used in the later XK120s, but those cars fitted with overdrive came with a JLE series unit. As before, close-ratio gears were available on special order. A Borg-Warner three-speed automatic transmission was introduced on the FHC in 1956. LHD models received them in January, while RHD examples were first fitted with the option in June.

The remote control switch for the optional Laycock de Normanville overdrive, which became available from late 1954. Unlike other British sports cars equipped with the same option, the Model 28/1390 unit worked on top gear only, allowing an overall ratio of 3:58:1.

The XK140 OTS used the same windscreen assembly as the XK120, though the early alloy-bodied cars had a larger rubber grommet at the bottom.

This prominent enamel badge replaced the growler emblem that had been affixed to the XK120's bonnet. It was attached directly to the modified grille assembly.

In profile, the XK140 DHC displays obvious similarities with its immediate predecessor, save for the more substantial bumpers and slightly enlarged cockpit dimensions.

With the hood stowed, the XK140 DHC featured a prominent bustle at the rear that suggested the appearance of a more substantial vehicle than the OTS.

Under the bonnet, all three variants were fitted with the same powerplant that had appeared in the XK120 SE, producing 190 bhp at 5,500 rpm. The unit was carried over essentially unchanged, save for measures introduced to save money or make production simpler, such as a smaller pressed steel oil sump, revised intake manifolds and a single exhaust system. A special equipment package was also made available similar to before, known as the SE kit in the home market and MC specification in the United States. It included adjustable fog lamps, windscreen washer jets, more comprehensive boot trim and chrome wire wheels.

An optional extra for SE specification models was the C-type cylinder head, which was fitted with increased diameter exhaust valves and had improved flow characteristics for better performance. It was supplied with SU H6 or larger H8 dual carburettors, an uprated crankshaft damper, revised ignition profile, twin exhaust silencers and pancake air filters, allowing the engine to produce 210 bhp at 5,750 rpm. An electric Laycock de Normanville overdrive unit was optional, while a Borg-Warner Model DG three-speed automatic transmission and a 3:54:1 rear axle ratio were offered from January 1956, completing the transformation from sports car to grand tourer for models so fitted.

To address overheating problems in warm weather conditions, a more efficient radiator appeared with a new cooling fan and water pump, which was repositioned to accommodate an Alford & Alder rack and pinion steering unit to replace the XK120's obsolescent Burman recirculating ball system. The new steering gear was attached to a new column that was positioned at an angle that was more comfortable for the driver to operate than the near-horizontal orientation that it had before.

Although the roadster and drophead coupé versions of the XK140 retained the same profile as their predecessors, the fixed-head coupé gained a roofline that was 6¾ inches longer and a windscreen frame that was moved forward, increasing the available cabin room despite the installation of wider doors and allowing for the provision of bigger side windows.

The larger cabin in the fixed-head coupé helped address the issue of limited interior space, a source of frequent criticism in its predecessor, but Jaguar liberated far more room when the front bulkhead was repositioned 3 inches forward. At the same time, the instrument panel was raised by an additional inch in the roadster and drophead coupé, while the scuttle assemblies in the roadster and fixed-head coupé were also repositioned, providing additional space in the footwells and promoting greater air circulation to reduce cabin temperatures.

With the additional cockpit space, made larger still with the use of thinner seatbacks and moving the batteries to a spot under the front wings, there was even room for a small pair of occasional rear seats. Although handsomely trimmed to match the rest of the interior surfaces, the small cushions had limited utility, except as a place to store soft luggage or to torture an unfortunate adult who, even then, had to sit sideways to fit in the tiny space.

The repositioned front bulkhead forced the engine forward by 3 inches, improving the vehicle's weight distribution to almost neutral, which reduced the propensity towards oversteer and provided better overall handling. More robust torsion bars, sourced from the XK120 SE, were fitted to all models, as were more durable Girling telescopic dampers at the rear in place of the old lever-arm units. The braking system remained the same, save for the adoption of a single master cylinder and a conventional handbrake in place of the fly-off version that had been used previously, though it soon returned after customers complained about the switch.

Popular Acclaim

From the XK140's introduction in 1954 and throughout the following year, sales were brisk, proving that the modifications implemented were effective in addressing the few concerns raised about its predecessor. In its first review of the model, *Road & Track* reported:

> With performance per dollar excelled by no other car, the nicer details of finish and fittings on the XK roadster come as a pleasant bonus feature. The quality of finish is immediately apparent on the outside, but a look under the hood shows attention to detail that is in marked contrast to that found under a domestic product.

Sports Cars Illustrated focused its comments on the comfort improvements:

> In the first place, and unquestionably most important, the 140 is a lot more comfortable than the 120. The engine has been moved forward and the cockpit considerably enlarged. This is a step in the right direction if you happen to be near the six-foot mark, because the old 120 just wouldn't let you get aboard with that much length. The wheel has been canted slightly too, and the whole revision adds up to a lot more enjoyable car to drive.

Over what would prove a relatively short production run, few running changes were made to the XK140. Most of them appeared in 1956, including the debut

The XK140 DHC featured a longer hood to account for the occasional rear seats, with a larger backlight than in the previous model. More luxurious than before, the hood assembly boasted walnut capping and more chrome trim.

From this perspective, the XK140 DHC can be visually distinguished from the roadster by the more substantial windscreen frame, taller doors and the stowed hood assembly.

A Hardura mat bound in Rexine covered the plywood floor in the boot. This example has been provided with special luggage designed to fit in the limited space available.

Unlike in the XK120, the spare tyre in the XK140 resided in a formed well that was covered with a plywood panel that hinged at the front. As seen here, the jack and tools were fastened with clips attached to the underside of the floor.

The cabin in the XK140 DHC boasted the same luxurious trappings that had been introduced for the XK120 DHC but with some variations in the size and shape of the various wood pieces.

The seatback cushions in the FHC were made thinner to maximise space for those unfortunate souls consigned to the occasional rear seats. Otherwise, the interior furnishings were the same as in the DHC.

In order to accommodate the occasional rear seats, the XK140 FHC introduced an extended roof made 6½ inches longer and 1½ inches taller. Few panels remained in common with the OTS and FHC, including the outer rear wings and boot area. Among the other styling changes introduced for this model were a windscreen moved farther forward, larger quarterlights, longer doors and shorter headlamp fairings.

The occasional rear seats in the FHC resembled those used in the DHC. The panel above the seats allowed access to the upper shelf in the boot.

Although superficially similar to the DHC, the FHC's doors were longer and featured a window with a vertical frame at the rear.

This view of the XK140 FHC shows off the model's longer roofline and revised backlight. The increased glass area afforded by the larger windows and quarterlights is easily seen from this perspective.

of the optional automatic transmission (fitted to almost 800 examples) and the use of steel rather than aluminium for the door skins on both coupé variants. The fly-off handbrake returned at the same time as a nod to weekend racers and rally enthusiasts. The year also saw William Lyons receive an honour that was overdue, gaining an investiture as a Knight Bachelor of the Most Excellent Order of the British Empire for his contributions to the country's automotive industry and export trade, allowing him to be known as Sir William for the rest of his life.

Even as the XK140 found itself on the verge of replacement, it continued to win plaudits from the automotive press, but the high praise could not compensate for a reduction in customer demand that saw sales fall by more than 1,400 units in 1956. Most of the decline was likely due to external factors, such as increased competition in the sports car market, the closure of the Suez Canal in the autumn and credit restrictions that were imposed to dampen rampant consumer spending in the United Kingdom. Even with the decline in sales for the XK140, however, increased demand for the saloon cars ensured Jaguar's continued profitability, though plans were already in the works for a more modern sports car to assume the XK mantle.

As before, the open two-seat roadster proved the most popular version of the XK140, accounting for 3,354 examples, compared to the 5,948 coupés that were built, almost evenly split between the fixed-head and drophead variants. Built from 1954 to 1957, the XK120 outsold the XK140 by 3,126, though this gap can be attributed to the latter's shorter production run. With a desirable blend of the original XK's timeless styling and a more practical and comfortable package, the XK140 remains one of the best classic cars to own and enjoy, offering much and demanding little in return.

A Hybrid Sensation

As 1956 drew to a close, it was clear that D-type sales had run their course. Despite continued competition success, only thirteen racecars had been delivered to customers that year, leaving twenty-nine examples still unsold at the factory. Borrowing a page from Ferrari, which had previously converted a number of prototypes into production sports cars by fitting them with minimal weather protection and other equipment required for legal road use, Jaguar endeavoured to do the same with the leftover D-types. Earlier that year, Duncan Hamilton had done much the same thing when he added a simple windshield and crude hood to an old D-type, creating a road-going version of the landmark racer at little cost.

Even better, a properly converted D-type could compete in the production category under SCCA rules in the United States, where Lyons hoped to sell the model to customers eager for a dual purpose sports car that could be driven to work and raced on the weekends. The changes necessary for the conversion to road use were minor, requiring no alteration to the existing

Steve McQueen bought his XKSS in 1958 from a local television personality in Los Angeles. Nicknamed the 'Green Rat' as a tribute to James Dean's 'Little Bastard,' the film star sold it after receiving too many speeding tickets but bought it back in 1977. (Jaguar Land Rover Heritage)

In commemoration of Jaguar's 75th anniversary in 2010, the Pebble Beach Concours d'Elegance assembled an XKSS exhibition featuring twelve of the sixteen surviving examples. (Jaguar Land Rover Heritage)

understructure or running gear, which allowed the prototype to be built in only three days.

The cockpit divider was eliminated to create more cabin space and the headrest was removed to create a more suitable civilian profile. Although nothing could be done about the compromised space in the passenger compartment, which was limited by the location of the dry sump reservoir and exhaust in front of the bulkhead, there were a number of improvements made to the cabin, including more comfortable seats, a passenger door and complete trim throughout the cockpit. A simple hood and side curtains offered some modest weather protection, while a wraparound windscreen, luggage rack and more substantial lighting completed the transformation to a passable road car that was known as the XKSS.

The first example was completed around 18 January 1957, allowing it to be shipped the following week to the United States, where it served as a demonstrator to stoke enthusiasm in the motoring press. Although it was too soon to gauge demand for the new model, production would have been limited to the number of remaining D-types in inventory, save for four examples that were disassembled for spare parts. Despite the weight of the added equipment and the aerodynamic penalty imposed by the proper windscreen, the performance on tap from the XKSS remained in the same class as the D-type, leading to a number of laudatory articles that should have allowed the entire production run to sell out. Unfortunately, fate had other plans and the number of cars actually constructed and sold was far fewer than first thought.

A Fiery Finish

Not long after the XKSS demonstrator arrived on American shores, a tragic fire struck Browns Lane on 12 February 1957. The conflagration started in the tyre stores and soon spread to the final assembly and service areas, gutting the completed and partially completed inventory of cars and destroying much of the structure. Despite the intensity of the flames and the thickening smoke, dedicated employees tried to save as many cars as they could, while even Sir William helped direct the fire brigade when they arrived at the factory gates.

Although the damage was mainly restricted to the area where testing and final assembly occurred, rather than the more vital section of the works such as the machine shop and engine assembly room, the incident impacted future plans and extracted a terrible financial cost, which was estimated at around £3.5 million. The extent of the loss forced an effective end to the XK140 and delayed the debut of its replacement until late spring, but sixteen examples of the rare XKSS survived (including the first car that had already arrived safely in New York). North American customers would account for fourteen of the sixteen units sold, the last pair being destined for London and Hong Kong. With so few

The aftermath of the conflagration at Browns Lane in 1957 forced a delay in the XK150's introduction and spared all but sixteen examples of the iconic XKSS. (Jaguar Land Rover Heritage)

examples on the market, they have become the most valuable Jaguars in the world, worth around £20 million or more when they exchange hands.

In an almost unprecedented move, Jaguar decided to manufacture an additional nine examples in 2016, representing the number that had been destroyed during the fire. Not surprisingly, given the passage of almost sixty years, almost all the tooling had to be recreated and over 10,000 man-hours were involved in the construction process. Sold at £1 million each, all were purchased by favoured customers, except for a solitary example that was retained by the factory.

Chapter 4
After the Fire

Lyons had originally wanted to replace the XK120 with a successor cloaked in more contemporary coachwork, abandoning the curvier lines, flared wings and cutaway doors in favour of an almost linear profile that hinted at the shape of the future S-type saloon. Progressing as far as the mock-up stage, it was pushed aside after Lyons determined that his company lacked the wherewithal to create the tooling that such a new model would require.

Modern styling for the XK series eventually arrived with the XK150, though the Browns Lane factory fire delayed its formal introduction until May 1957. While some marque enthusiasts may have hoped for an entirely new platform, Jaguar lacked the resources at the time for such a manifest change, resulting in retention of the existing chassis and running gear but cloaking them with fashionable bodywork that was a complete departure from the previous models.

The most obvious difference between the XK150 and its predecessors came from the new body, which incorporated a more subtle Lyons Line with a higher waistline, more fully integrated envelope bodywork and smoother, but somewhat better endowed, contours. Although retaining some recognisable styling elements from the original XK120, most of its traditional design cues were abandoned, such as the hint of separate wings, divided windscreen, powerful haunches and the sweeping character line that plunged towards the rear wheel arch. In truth, the XK150's more bulbous shape bore a greater resemblance to the compact saloon range than to its distinguished forebears, but enough familiarity remained for the casual observer to ascertain its lineage without much trouble.

A fuller bonnet, broader at the base, was set between the fuller front wings, stamped with a centreline rib that ran forward from the raised scuttle to a widened radiator grille, which more closely approximated the shape used on the 2.4-litre saloon. Much of the new design's modernity flowed from the wraparound windscreen, especially in the fixed-head coupé where the curved glass matched the roof's contours much better than the flat panes and divided frame used in the XK120 and XK140. The full effect of the frontal styling suggested a much larger and wider vehicle, emphasised by the new grille, wider façade and re-contoured front bumper. At the back, a more substantial single-piece bumper, larger number plate surround and a broader, flatter tail section festooned with additional brightwork appeared, making the rear aspect appear more luxurious but also busier than the XK120's austere tail. Except for the bonnet and boot lid, which were crafted from aluminium, all of the new panels were made from steel.

Grace, Pace and More Space

When first introduced, only the fixed-head and drophead coupés were made available for purchase, meaning that roadster enthusiasts would have to wait until it could be readied for production. The new body, principally the slimmer doors and higher scuttle, liberated a good deal of additional space inside the cabin, including an extra 4 inches of shoulder room. Particularly in the fixed-head coupé, where the roof was raised and made flatter in shape, there was an almost saloon car feel to the entire cabin. The more generous roof structure also made it possible to incorporate a larger backlight for better rearward visibility and more light.

The drophead coupé retained a similar hood to that used in the XK140 but the bustle that was created when it was stowed appeared more prominent, degrading somewhat the smoother lines of the new bodywork. The opening vent windows appended to the new windshield frame were somewhat incongruous in appearance, though they were certainly welcome in hot climates when any fresh air was welcome indeed.

Marking a significant departure from previous practice, walnut wood veneer trim inside the cabin was replaced with leathercloth on the instrument panel, fascia, dash top and doors, although some of the earliest examples featured instrument panels with polished aluminium trim. The instrument layout was

From any vantage point the XK150 offers a more modern appearance, with fuller coachwork and a curved windscreen. Underneath, the same basic understructure and running gear were utilised as before.

Sir William Lyons believed that success at Le Mans boosted sales, accounting for this badge detailing the marque's victories at the Circuit de la Sarthe.

Because the XK150 OTS lacked the occasional rear seats fitted in the DHC and FHC, the forward bulkhead was moved 4 inches back and the bonnet made longer as a result. Note the longer rear deck compared to the previous editions.

The XK150 was the first OTS variant equipped with rollup windows.

Although the standard specification power plant carried over from the XK140, most XK150s were fitted with the SE engine with the B-type cylinder head used in the contemporary Mark VIII and 3.4-litre saloons. The improved cylinder head increased output to 210 bhp at 5,500 rpm and 216 pound-feet of torque at 3,000 rpm. Note that the cowl for the radiator fan has been removed in this example. The rare S package featured an improved straight-port cylinder designed by Harry Weslake. It offered 250 bhp at 5,500 rpm and 240 pound-feet of torque at 4,500 rpm.

Despite a different switch than in the previous model, the Laycock de Normanville overdrive unit fitted to the XK150 remained unchanged, operating on the top gear with a 28 per cent reduction offered. The warning lamp for low brake fluid and handbrake engagement is barely visible to the left of the steering wheel hub.

The XK150 front bumper featured an indentation that conformed to the shape of the grille. Note the splash apron fitted behind the bumper and the Lucas J.700 headlamps. (John Goodman)

Displaying strong familial traits with Jaguar's contemporary saloons, the XK150's modernity is seen to best advantage in the FHC. The curved windscreen and generous greenhouse make this a particularly attractive example of the breed.

There was more room available in the XK150 than ever before thanks to redesigned doors and slimmer seat cushions. The entire layout was more modern and contemporary due to the absence of wood trim. The Nardi steering wheel fitted here is a period accessory.

Both the FHC and DHC used the same occasional rear seats for the first time, though there was still not enough room to make them an attractive proposition for actual humans.

This iconic leaper was an optional extra.

The fascia followed the layout used in the contemporary saloons but the luxurious walnut veneer from previous models was replaced with leathercloth, though alloy appeared in some very early examples.

carried over from the compact saloons, further emphasising the similarities among the models, though there were some detail differences. Wider seats were also introduced to take advantage of the extra cabin width, with a padded armrest placed over the tunnel for the propeller shaft. The seats were hinged to allow access to the occasional rear seats but bucket seats remained an option, though it was rarely specified despite their comfort and attractive appearance. The remainder of the interior trim was far more contemporary than in the XK140, featuring fewer embellishments than before but still managing to look suitably luxurious for a car of such obvious class.

Under the bonnet, the previous engine used in the XK140 remained as standard equipment, supplying a still healthy 190 bhp at 5,500 rpm, but it was supplemented with a more powerful unit for the Special Equipment models. This optional power plant was fitted with the new B-type cylinder head that was fitted with larger exhaust valves and improved gas flow, as well as an improved intake manifold with a separate water gallery for more consistent operating temperatures. Fitted with SU HD6 carburettors, the uprated engine produced 210 bhp at 5,500 rpm and 216 pound-feet of torque at 3,000 rpm.

As before, the transmission options were the standard gearbox from Moss, available with electric overdrive, or the optional Borg-Warner three-speed automatic, which was now operated from a central dashboard-mounted lever that accommodated both left and right-hand steering. The chassis was little different, but for the addition of an extra pair of outriggers and changes to the various brackets, while the suspension and steering was identical except for the addition of nylon chafing gear between the leaf springs and rubber insulation for the steering gear.

A New Sensation

Of course, the most significant improvement for the XK150 was the introduction of four-wheel disc brakes, making it one of the very first cars to offer the revolutionary technology, being beaten to market only by the Triumph TR3, which still retained drums at the back, and the very limited production Austin-Healey 100S and Jensen 541S. The system was developed in cooperation with Dunlop and successfully tested on Jaguar's sports racers at Le Mans, which had used them to good effect in 1953, 1955 and 1956 (and would do so again in June 1957) by winning the prestigious race against the celebrated competition from Cunningham, Mercedes-Benz and Ferrari.

The innovative brakes were part of the SE package, which was fitted to the majority of the XK150s built. Perhaps the explanation for why so many cars were fitted with this optional package comes down to the presence of the disc brakes as part of the kit, owing to the great advantage they provided in reducing unsprung weight and increasing overall braking capacity.

The Dunlop system featured 12-inch rotors at all four corners operated by a single pair of pistons fitted with unique round brake pads, assisted by a Lockheed vacuum servo unit, supplied with pressure from the intake manifold. Because the

New lighting requirements that appeared toward the end of the 1950s forced adoption of this larger rear light cluster with a separate reflector lens in late 1959.

The XK150 boot layout was the same as before, with the spare tyre housed in a separate compartment beneath a hinged floorboard.

This view of a 1958 XK150 FHC shows the larger backlight and the more substantial full-width rear bumper that appeared with this model. Compare the size of the rear light clusters with those fitted to the 1960 XK150 DHC presented below.

From this perspective, the XK150 DHC provides a glimpse of the future that would arrive with the Jensen Interceptor and Aston Martin DBS, combining sports car potency with the luxury and isolation that only a proper grand touring car can provide. Although the hood bustle is a distraction to the flowing lines, it is a necessary evil to achieve the desired comfort.

The veneered instrument panel is an owner addition, but the Bluemel four-spoke steering wheel is original. Note the aftermarket radio fitted below the fascia.

The instrument panel was common to all three XK150 variants. The fascia covering matched the seat trim, with most of the controls carried over from the XK140, although the wiper knob was new. The instruments themselves were revised and the needles provided with red tips.

The XK150's frontal styling was more complicated than in the first XK120, especially with the addition of driving lights, as shown here.

The XK150 DHC adopted a side window with a more angular shape than the curved glass used in the OTS. Note the opening vent window that appeared only in the DHC and FHC versions.

The XK150 DHC shared the same occasional rear seats as the FHC. Note the absence of legroom that rendered the seats rather impractical for their intended purpose.

The XK150 retained the same Moss gearbox used in the XK140, with the Borg-Warner three-speed transmission available as an option. When fitted with the latter, it was operated from a small lever positioned beneath the fascia that accommodated both left and right-hand drive examples.

Although the XK150 DHC's large hood bustle is a visual distraction, there is no doubt that the entire package is far more modern than before.

With the hood raised, the XK150 is particularly attractive, presenting a dignified profile that fits in well with the rest of the Jaguar range.

calipers had to be dismantled to change the pads, the company soon adopted the quick-change square pads that were developed for the D-type sports racer.

In his preview of the new model, *Autosport*'s John Bolster wrote:

> ... the Jaguar XK150 goes a stage further towards realizing the modern ideal of the sports car ... The new Jaguar is immensely fast, one need hardly remark, but it is more roomy and practical as an everyday vehicle than its predecessors, with improved all-round visibility and a distinctly Continental line. On the mechanical side, the engine has better low and medium speed torque, which increases the already excellent top gear flexibility, but most important of all is the adoption of disc brakes, which really permit the full performance to be exploited.

Unusually, the majority of the cars produced were built to SE specification, consisting of the B-type cylinder head, disc brakes, wire wheels and windscreen washers, which is the first time that the performance package proved more popular than the standard model. This curious trend remained true after the open two-seat roadster was announced in March 1958, arriving after the two coupé variants for several reasons likely related to competing projects and the aftermath of the fire.

Because the roadster lacked the occasional rear seats fitted to the fixed-head and drophead coupé, there was more space in the cabin, resulting in a somewhat modified bodyshell that had the scuttle and windscreen moved 4 inches to the rear. This change required a longer bonnet, which made the entire package seem more sensual, possessing proportions that were more visually appealing with the long front and short back.

Inarguably the most attractive of the XK150 variants, due in large part to the absence of the bustle required for the drophead coupé and the lack of rear seats, the roadster offered a lower profile, emphasised by the smoother, longer rear deck. For the first time in an open two-seat XK model, rollup windows were available, set off with distinctive chrome frames for the glass and on the door caps. Moreover, the hood featured a more elegant profile when erected, made possible by a revised frame assembly that was also simpler to operate. The new hood also possessed a larger backlight, making it less claustrophobic to drive when it was erected.

When the roadster debuted to the public at the New York Motor Show following its earlier introduction to the press, Jaguar announced that export customers would be provided the opportunity to order an improved engine as part of the S performance package (initially available only on the open two-seater). In order to compensate for the added weight that came with the XK150's new bodyshell and more comprehensive kit, Sir William turned again to Harry Weslake, who performed his usual magic in reworking the existing cylinder head to achieve greater efficiency and more power.

The 'straight port' head that Weslake designed took advantage of more efficient gas flow, especially at higher engine revolutions. The new cylinder head arrived with a host of important internal modifications to the engine, including an increased 9:1 compression ratio, more durable bearings and lightened reciprocal mass. Also added were new intake and exhaust manifolds that could accommodate a dramatic addition – triple 2-inch SU HD8 carburettors! The end results of these modifications and additions were improved responsiveness and increased tractability throughout the power band, making exceptional use of the available 250 bhp at 5,500 rpm and 240 pound-feet of torque at 4,500 rpm.

Until superseded by an even more improved S version in 1959, these were the fastest cars of the XK series, with acceleration from a stop to 60 mph in 7.3 seconds and a 136 mph top speed, numbers that *Road & Track* admitted 'speak for themselves'.

In a test from Australia's *Sports Car World*, the XK150S was described as a 'supremely attractive car with all the power, both going and stopping that most enthusiasts could want', while John Bolster wrote for *Autosport*:

> The acceleration figures are, of course, stupendous ... To cover a standing quarter-mile in 15.8 secs., or to accelerate from a standstill to 100 m.p.h. in 20 secs. is to unleash a surge of power that the average motorist can hardly visualize. These figures would be expected of a sports-racing car, but to obtain them from an extremely comfortable and well-equipped closed vehicle is an astonishing experience.

From October 1958 both the fixed-head and drophead coupés could be ordered in 'S' specification but the real news was the increased displacement 3.8-litre engine that would be offered in both standard and 'S' trim. With an actual displacement of 3,781cc, achieved by increasing the bore from 83 mm to 87 mm, it produced 220 bhp at 5,500 rpm and 240 pound-feet at 3,000 rpm in standard tune.

More importantly from a performance perspective, however, the new engine made an astounding 265 bhp at 5,500 rpm and 260 pound-feet of torque at 4,000 rpm when provided with the S specification equipment. Although the stopwatch numbers were not significantly improved by the extra displacement, the engine was far more refined and tractable, capable of propelling the car to exceptional speeds when the throttle pedal was depressed.

By 1960, plans for the XK150's replacement had been underway for several years but the old warhorse was set to soldier on for a while longer. With the coming of the new decade, new governmental regulations forced some changes, including a larger, more complicated rear lamp cluster with separate reflectors. With the E-type already in the final stages of development, there were few substantive alterations made to what was still an excellent vehicle, but there was no denying that its successor was a quantum leap forward on several fronts. The final XK150 left Browns Lane in January 1961, leaving a gap that would remain unfilled until the E-type was formally introduced in Switzerland in March. For a long time, the XK150 would exist in a twilight world, less recognised than the original XK120 and not as outwardly spectacular as the world-class E-type that followed it. In more recent years, it has received a more favourable reappraisal, accounting for a significant increase in both resale values and interest. With 9,385 sold, the XK150 may have sold 2,676 fewer than the first model in the series, but it will long be remembered as the most sophisticated example of the breed.

Sir William Lyons standing before an assemblage of his company's products during the 1960s. (Graham Robson Collection)

Chapter 5
The XK in Competition

Unlike some of his automotive contemporaries such as David Brown, Colin Chapman, Donald Healey and Enzo Ferrari, who viewed racing as a natural part of the business, Sir Williams Lyons considered it a mere tool to boost sales of his production cars. Complicating matters for those that yearned to hear the name of the Coventry automaker uttered in the same breath as Alfa Romeo, Ferrari, Maserati and Mercedes-Benz, he was also hesitant to enter any race that his cars could not win, wanting to avoid any potential embarrassment that might ensue from the failure of a dedicated factory effort.

There was certainly a great deal on the line for Jaguar, especially since the XK120 held the record as the world's fastest production car after the run at Jabbeke on 30 May 1949. In order to test the new sports car's racing mettle, an example was successfully track tested for more than three hours, providing Lyons with the confidence to authorise a trio of XK120s to contest an upcoming BRDC event at Silverstone later that summer. Although all three cars were technically privateers,

Although various pre-war models were campaigned on the international stage, including an overall victory for the SS100 on the 1936 Coupes Internationals des Alpes, the XK120 propelled Jaguar into the first rank among the world's sports car manufacturers. (Jaguar Land Rover Heritage)

Much of the XX120's competition success can be attributed to the extremely robust chassis, reliable powerplant and predictable handling. The only weakness that it displayed was a disturbing propensity for the brakes to fade under repeated use, which Jaguar soon remedied in its sports racers. (Jaguar Land Rover Heritage)

they were factory prepared and assigned drivers that had been specially selected for the task. Despite stiff competition from an Allard, Frazer-Nash and Healey during the race, Leslie Johnson and Peter Walker finished in first and second place, providing the XK120 with an auspicious maiden outing.

Sowing the Seeds

Still uncertain whether a formal works team was really worth all the effort, Jaguar procured a half-dozen hand-assembled alloy examples for use by selected privateers, though the cars were specially prepared and received significant factory support. Among the earliest forays were a fifth overall at the 1950 Mille Miglia and a third at the Circuit of Oporto, but the 24 Hours of Le Mans during the summer was even more momentous. Although listed as private entrants, Leslie Johnson, Bert Hadley, Nick Haines, Peter Clark, John Marshall and Peter Whitehead operated as an unofficial works team, driving under the supervision of F. R. W. 'Lofty' England, who ran the service department at Browns Lane.

In a pattern that many British manufacturers followed at the time, the cars ran in essentially unmodified form, carefully assembled and maintained to be sure, but running with the same weight and power output as the standard models. Despite this performance handicap and brakes that deteriorated noticeably as the race wore on, the XK120 proved itself a match for the fastest cars in the world, finishing twelfth and fifteenth overall. The accomplishment would have been even more impressive but Leslie Johnson retired with a broken clutch while running second overall with three hours left, having been forced to slow the car with the transmission rather than the failing brakes.

Propitiously, Lyons and Heynes watched the race from the pits, allowing them to see the XK120's racing potential for themselves. The performance of the relatively stock examples dispelled the persistent myth that success at Le Mans required special tuning, tremendous financial resources and technical gimmickry. Instead, having watched what near stock examples could achieve in the hands of talented drivers, Heynes felt that the basic platform could win with more aerodynamic bodywork and less weight to haul around. After all, the less technically advanced entrants from Allard and Healey had finished in third and fourth position thanks in large part to their aerodynamically efficient shapes, making it apparent that an XK120 with a similar profile could benefit similarly. Most importantly, Lyons gave Heynes full authority to build a dedicated sports racer based on these principles, which would appear the following year as the XK120C but became much better known as the C-type.

The month after the XK120's success at the Circuit de la Sarthe, Ian Appleyard secured a class win and a Coupes des Alpes in the Alpine Rally, seated alongside his wife and navigator Patricia Lyons, who was the chairman's daughter. Proving

Despite its privateer status with owner Ian Appleyard, NUB 120 boasts the most successful competition pedigree for the model. Barely missing out on a win in its maiden outing at the 1950 Tulip Rally, it received a Coupes des Alpes at the 1950 Alpine Rally, followed by a string of additional victories at the RAC and Tulip rallies. It repeated its success in the French Alps the next year and then won a Gold Cup before retiring in 1953. (Jaguar Land Rover Heritage)

80

The XK120 had a formidable racing reputation in North America, fuelled by innumerable successful outings. Among them were Phil Hill's outright victory at the 1950 Pebble Beach Cup and SCCA national championships in 1952, 1954 and 1955. (British Sports Car Hall of Fame)

Ordered specifically for competition use with sandcast carburettors and an uprated gearbox, this example contested Liége–Rome–Liége on three consecutive outings from 1952 to 1954. It finished an impressive eleventh overall in its maiden effort. (Jaguar Land Rover Heritage)

Another example that illustrates the XK120's success as a privateer mount, LOE 409 finished well in a number of domestic rallies and speed trials, and secured a second overall at the Rallye Soleil Cannes in 1951. It later competed in the United States at club level. (REVS Library)

the most successful of the XK120 rally teams, Appleyard and Lyons repeated their feat in two subsequent Alpines and also recorded victories at the RAC and Tulip rallies.

Meanwhile, the XK120 continued to rack up other wins, including the International Trophy at Silverstone and an overall win at the Tourist Trophy in Ireland, the latter with Stirling Moss at the wheel, which would prove decisive in his recruitment for the official factory racing team that was taking shape. Even after the calendar turned to 1951, more success followed at Liége–Rome–Liége and the Scottish Rally, although a return to Le Mans was overshadowed by the C-type's appearance.

Despite the arrival of the celebrated sports racer, the XK120 competed in numerous races and rallies, winning SCCA national championships in 1952, 1954 and 1955 and amassing victories in exotic locales like East Africa, Finland and Singapore. The model remained a fixture in club racing events throughout the following decade, finding later success on the vintage racing circuit.

Although the XK140 never recorded the same competition success as its illustrious predecessor and the iconic sports racers, Robert Walshaw and Peter Bolton completed 209 laps at the 1956 24 Hours of Le Mans, only to be disqualified over an alleged refuelling infraction with only three hours left in the race. Among the highlights for the XK140 were class wins at the 1955 Scottish Rally and the 1956 Mille Miglia, along with another SCCA national championship almost a decade later, proving that life remained in the old platform.

By the time that the XK150 arrived on the scene, road racing at the highest levels was no longer possible given the dedicated sports racers, while success on the rally circuit had become the province of much smaller vehicles. Nonetheless, surprises still happened, such as a class win at the 1960 Tulip Rally and a podium finish at an SCCA national event in the United States, but the XK150 would find more action as a club racer in later years, primarily in marque events.

AJK 48 competed in the BARC Eastbourne Rally, Rallye International Evian-Mont Blanc, Prescott Hill Climb, Brighton Speed Trials and on the road circuit at Goodwood. It also appeared in a 1957 feature film called *The Truth About Women*. (Jaguar Land Rover Heritage)

Stanley Boshier leads Mark Levy at Goodwood in 1952. Boshier started his racing career in a Healey Silverstone before purchasing an XK120 in 1951. He would win races at Snetterton and Fersfield in the car. (Jaguar Land Rover Heritage)

An XK120 awaiting departure from a checkpoint during the Rallye International Evian-Mont Blanc on 28 July 1951. The first event was held in 1947, established to promote the famous mineral water brand. It underwent several name and route changes before becoming the Rallye Mont-Blanc-Morzine in 1961. (Jaguar Land Rover Heritage)

Roy Salvadori racing an XK120 at Silverstone on 24 May 1952. He finished in second place, only 1.2 seconds behind the Alta Jaguar that won the race. (Jaguar Land Rover Heritage)

David Hobbs started his thirty-year motorsports career in this 1955 Jaguar XK140, which he drove while serving an apprenticeship at Daimler. He would go on to compete in several racing series, including Formula One, NASCAR, IMSA, Can-Am and Trans-Am, finishing third at the 24 Hours of Le Mans in 1969 and 1984. (Jaguar Land Rover Heritage)

C for Competition

Work on a dedicated sports racer using the running gear from the XK120 started in late 1950, aiming to produce a vehicle with less weight and better handling and braking than the production model it was based on. Built to win at Le Mans, the C-type made Jaguar's reputation as a performance marque to be reckoned with, a position that it still holds more six decades later.

Although most of the hardware came from the XK120, it was an entirely different beast from its production sibling. William Heynes designed a lightweight multi-tubular triangulated frame structure built upon a base formed from robust channel-section frame members. Although the size of the tubes varied, the entire structure was made more rigid with a welded panel scuttle and an additional bulkhead attached to the chassis.

The front suspension was sourced from the XK120 using unequal length wishbones and longitudinal torsion bars, while the rear suspension was built to a new design featuring a rigid axle suspended on a single transverse torsion bar secured with a trailing link at each end. In an effort to improve on the XK120's notoriously inferior braking performance, Lockheed self-adjusting 12-inch brake drums were installed at all four corners. Rack and pinion steering was also fitted to make the helm easier to operate for a full day's running, as were 16-inch alloy wire wheels to save weight.

A Jaguar C-type surrounded by the proud members of the competition department at Foleshill. Of the fifty-three examples built from 1951 to 1953, all but ten were sold to privateers who campaigned them with varying levels of factory support and involvement. (Jaguar Land Rover Heritage)

A true workhorse, OKC 011 finished ninth overall for Ecurie Francorchamps at the 1953 24 Hours of Le Mans and also ran that same year at the Spa 24-Hours and Nurburgring 1,000-Kilometres. It was sold to Dunlop as a developmental mule before entering long-term private ownership. Bonhams sold the car at auction in 2016 for £5,715,580. (REVS Library)

Power came from the familiar XK engine, but suitably modified with larger exhaust valves, higher lift camshafts, an 8:1 compression ratio and larger dual SU H8 carburettors, producing 200 bhp at 5,800 rpm. The Moss gearbox was carried over from the XK120, offering reliable and robust, rather than smooth, operation. It was mated to a Borg & Beck 10-inch dry plate clutch and a Hardy Spicer propeller shaft that led to a hypoid bevel final drive unit.

In order to maximise the C-type's speed down the Mulsanne Straight, Malcolm Sayer designed an aerodynamic body with much smoother contours and a lower profile than the traditionally styled XK120 and its significant frontal area. Decades before computer aided drafting entered the engineering lexicon, Sayer pioneered its use in automotive design without having had access to an actual computer, relying only on a slide rule and some log tables to perform the complex mathematical calculations required. Oddly, he had learned the basic process from a German engineering professor who had taught him that three-dimensional objects could be designed arithmetically, using numbers alone to divine the optimal shape to cheat the wind.

For Sayer, who had learned his trade at the Bristol Aeroplane Company during the war, that meant a bodyshell that required the minimal amount of horsepower to achieve a target speed, constrained only by the dimensions of the underlying chassis and powertrain. While everything that he touched was undeniably beautiful, perhaps a nod to his patron's overall styling influence and practiced eye, Sayer insisted that he was an aerodynamicist rather than an automotive stylist.

The envelope bodyshell that he designed was fashioned entirely from aluminium and consisted of a hinged front section that allowed uncompromised access to the engine and a rear section that could be quickly removed to reach the rear suspension and the after framework. Although not as efficient as the later D-type, the new shape was a vast improvement over the XK120, which became apparent after extensive testing at Silverstone and the test track at MIRA.

All that remained was to prove the design in actual competition at the Circuit de la Sarthe, which saw a trio of examples depart from Coventry for the long drive and ferry ride to France in June 1951. In order to compete against the Aston Martins, Cunninghams, Ferraris, Nash-Healeys and Talbot-Lagos on the grid, Jaguar arranged an impressive driving stable that included Stirling Moss in his first appearance at Le Mans and three-time Mille Miglia winner Clemente Biondetti, not to mention old hands Leslie Johnson, Peter Walker and Peter Whitehead who had won with impressive regularity with the standard XK120 in recent years.

As with any debut for a new racing model, problems were inevitable, but the vehicular trio started well and were running in the first three places not long after the start. Disaster struck the Biondetti and Johnson entry in the fifth hour, however, when an oil delivery pipe failed and forced them from the race. Not long afterwards, Moss and Fairman also fell out when low oil pressure caused a connecting rod to fail

Peter Walker and Peter Whitehead piloted XKC 003 to an overall victory at the 24 Hours of Le Mans in 1951 to set in motion the marque's dominance at the legendary event over the coming years. (Jaguar Land Rover Heritage)

after the same pipe problem occurred in their car. But even as the Jaguars had their run of ill fortune, so too did others in the gruelling competition. Difficulties with cooling caused the two leading Talbot-Lagos to retire as the race progressed, which left the lead to Walker and Whitehead in the remaining C-type.

The pair continued to cover ground with remarkable consistency through to the finish on the following afternoon, allowing Britain to secure its first win at Le Mans since 1935 with an unassailable lead over the Talbot-Lago T26 and Aston Martin DB2 that placed second and third. More so than the national honours at stake, it was a signal victory for Jaguar, placing the marque in the conversation as builders of the finest sports cars in the world. It was an amazing accomplishment for a company that only twenty years earlier had released an automobile of its own design.

Later that year, the C-type repeated the success achieved at Le Mans with Moss and Walker taking the first two spots at the RAC Tourist Trophy in their C-types, which was followed by yet another triumph for Moss at Goodwood. The following year, Jaguar had begun to experiment with disc brakes, using a Dunlop system that was intended to banish the company's braking problems once and for all. Testing a C-type with the new brakes, Moss finished fourth in a race at Goodwood in the spring, followed by a disappointingly poor outing at the Mille Miglia with Norman Dewis along for the ride.

After the Mille Miglia, Moss complained that more speed was necessary to repeat the previous year's success at Le Mans, resulting in a last-minute effort to fit more aerodynamic coachwork to the three cars, which was finished shortly before the cars departed for France. Unfortunately, the revised bodies required smaller radiators, causing cooling problems that forced two of the three works entries to retire in the early hours, while the last car succumbed around the same time due to low oil pressure.

After the disappointment of 1952, Jaguar returned again the following year, but the C-types had reverted to the original body style to eliminate the cooling difficulties and high-speed instability that had been encountered with the more aerodynamic coachwork. Although they looked the same as the 1951 models, the bodies were fashioned from thinner aluminium to save weight while additional savings came from using thinner gauge steel for certain chassis tubes and a rubber container for the fuel tank.

Output from the XK engine was improved to 220 bhp by replacing the dual SU H8 carburettors with triple DCO3 Weber units and a new rear suspension appeared, but the most significant change came from the installation of Dunlop disc brakes at all four corners. With far more stopping power than the drums used before, drivers could brake later, which was a significant advantage at a course with such high speeds and sharp corners.

The effect of the lighter weight, additional power and improved braking delivered a result that helped sustain a run of unprecedented success at Le Mans for a single marque. Finishing first, second and fourth overall, Tony Rolt and Duncan Hamilton piloted the winner at an average speed of 105.841 mph, the first time that a car had completed the gruelling race maintaining an average above 100 mph. Almost as impressive, the pair set a record for the distance covered with more than 2,500 miles in the books, further burnishing a wholly dominant performance for the legendary cats.

With all but ten of the fifty-three C-types built sold to privateers, it was natural that they would record most of the model's victories, none more successful than Écurie Ecosse which, along with other private entrants, helped Jaguar sustain a serious push for the 1953 Worlds Sports Car Championship, finishing second to Ferrari. Although the D-type arrived the following year, the C-type continued to accrue wins off the main stage, helping to cement its place in Jaguar lore.

Faster Pussycat

Not long after Jaguar recorded its second victory at Le Mans in three years, Heynes set out to ensure a successful reprise, convinced that more power and higher speeds were necessary to stay ahead of the competition. As had been the case with the C-type, created as the Mk VII was readied for market, development of its successor occurred while the company was labouring to produce its first saloon with monocoque construction, which would debut as the Mk I in 1955.

Extracting more power from the existing XK power plant was a relatively straightforward task, accomplished by modifications to the cylinder head, carburettor induction system, camshafts, valve train and a dry sump lubrication system, which produced almost 250 bhp at 5,750 rpm. As impressive as this was, something more was necessary to reach the speeds that were now required to win as the competition continued to make their own advancements.

What transpired was a radical departure from the previous car, representing a quantum technological leap that incorporated valuable lessons learned from the aviation industry and Jaguar's own experience with the Mk I saloon. Other than the live rear axle, almost everything under the skin of the new sports racer was state of the art and much more compact than in the C-type, featuring a central monocoque chassis section crafted from magnesium alloy, which was braced by sturdy fore and aft bulkheads that imparted even more rigidity to the affair. In the front, a complex fully welded aluminium tube frame, shaped like an arrow, and made as small as possible to reduce air resistance, carried the engine, suspension and steering.

As the project progressed, aerodynamic advantage was seen as the keystone to success, placing much of the credit for the D-type's ultimate success again in Sayer's lap. Unlike its illustrious predecessor, which was styled with an intentional familial resemblance to the XK120 to boost sales, the D-type was designed from a clean sheet to maximize its speed at Le Mans.

The result was a smaller, lower car, riding on a wheelbase that was almost 6 inches shorter than the C-type, with a much smaller frontal area. Relying heavily on his previous experience working for the Bristol Aeroplane Company, where he had specialized in the application of aerodynamic principles to mechanical design, Sayer continually refined the shape, even adding a vertical fin behind the driver's seat only weeks before the race after testing showed that it would improve straight line stability.

Norman Dewis, Jaguar's chief test driver and development engineer, sits behind the wheel of the D-type prototype as William Lyons and company cast their approval from alongside. (Jaguar Land Rover Heritage)

Chassis number XKC 401 took to the road on 13 April 1954, the first of a fine breed that would win the 24 Hours of Le Mans from 1955 to 1957. It is seen here in May 1954 during testing at the Motor Industry Research Association (MIRA) facility in Warwickshire. (Graham Robson Collection)

90

A Bitter Win

As before, the works recruited six talented drivers to pilot the cars for the 1954 race at the Circuit de la Sarthe: Hamilton and Rolt, Whitehead and Ken Wharton, and Moss and Walker. Intent on beating the reigning champion, Ferrari arrived with the new Tipo 375, powered by a 4.9-litre V-12 that produced an astounding 345 bhp. However, thanks to its superior aerodynamics and small frontal area, the D-type's top speed was higher and the race was widely seen as a contest between Jaguar's finesse and Ferrari's brute strength.

After driving through atrocious weather and surviving early fuel starvation problems that forced unforeseen pit time to remove blocked fuel filters, Moss and Walker retired at the halfway point with brake failure and shortly thereafter Whitehead and Wharton dropped out due to gearbox problems. The Ferraris also had their problems, as two out of three factory-entered cars also dropped out, and in the end the race was decided not by time on the track, but by time in the pits: 37 minutes for Jaguar versus only 29 for Ferrari. After 24 hours of racing, the only works D-type to finish was just 1 minute 45 seconds behind the only factory-backed Ferrari.

Even though the outright victory had eluded them, the new car performed well and seemed poised to win the next year. The works cars were further improved with longer noses for better aerodynamics, and power was increased to almost 275 bhp with additional cylinder head improvements and exhaust system modifications. These changes made possible a theoretical 183 mph top speed, which could prove decisive on the 3.7-mile-long straight at Le Mans, where the return of Mercedes-Benz made for a three-way rivalry between England, Italy and Germany, setting the stage for an epic battle combining national pride and marque loyalty.

Again the company fielded a three-car team, but with two new crews. In the lead car, British Formula One driver Mike Hawthorn, replacing Moss who had joined Mercedes, was paired with Ivor Bueb, while the second car was reserved for Don Beauman and the company's development engineer, Norman Dewis. The only returnees, Rolt and Hamilton, were placed in the third example.

Hawthorn and Bueb went on to win the race after the other two works Jaguars dropped out, but it was a sombre victory as this race is most remembered for the worst motor racing accident in history. At 6:20 p.m., on just the thirty-fifth lap of a race where the winning car could be expected to exceed 300 laps in total, Hawthorn was called in to the pits. As he approached the exit he overtook a slower car, an Austin-Healey 100S driven by Lance Macklin, whom he passed and then slowed to enter the pits.

All the evidence appears to indicate that, perhaps because he was looking in his mirror at the time, for a fatal fraction of a second Macklin failed to notice that the Jaguar had pulled in front of him. Noticing the danger immediately ahead, Macklin hit the brakes hard and his car swerved to the left, directly in front of the much faster Mercedes 300 SLR driven by Pierre Levegh, who clipped the Healey and was propelled airborne, where it flipped repeatedly toward the crowd.

The helpless Levegh was thrown clear and was killed on impact, while his car hit an embankment and disintegrated, spewing flaming bits of the engine, chassis and suspension into the crowd, where more than eighty spectators were killed and another 100 or more injured. Fearing that cancellation of the race would fill the road with departing spectators and impede the arrival of ambulances and access to local hospitals, race officials let the contest continue. However, out of both respect for the magnitude of the disaster and the desire to avoid adverse publicity, the Mercedes team quietly withdrew from the race in the middle of the night, even as they were holding the first and third positions overall, with Hawthorn's Jaguar in second.

By this time both of the works Ferraris had retired with mechanical ailments, leaving Jaguar with an unassailable lead ... if they could keep running. Approximately 16 hours into the race, the gearbox of the Rolt-Hamilton car seized, while the D-type driven by Beauman and Dewis got stuck in the sand when the former had an off-track excursion. Eventually, Hawthorn and Bueb motored on to finish five laps ahead of the second place Aston Martin. However, with all of their real competition – the Ferraris and Mercedes SLRs – out of the race, and the carnage of the horrific accident, Jaguar's third victory at Le Mans was a decidedly joyless one.

Mercedes withdrew from motorsport at the end of the 1955 season, an exile that would last for almost four decades, but Jaguar returned to Le Mans in 1956 in the hope that it could secure an untarnished victory for the D-type. It did not go as planned.

On only the second lap, Paul Frère, driving one of the factory cars, lost control in the Esses and hit the wall, causing his teammate Jack Fairman, who was following closely behind, to take evasive action. In doing so, however, Fairman

Chassis number XKD 404 was the third works car completed after the prototype D-type was built. It failed to complete the 1954 24 Hours of Le Mans due to a broken gearbox, but returned soon afterwards to win the 12-hour race at Reims. It served as the factory demonstrator and test mule before entering private ownership, where it won the 1960 Angolan Grand Prix. (Graham Robson Collection)

Despite the horrific accident that took the lives of more than eighty spectators, Mike Hawthorn and Ivor Bueb celebrate their victory at the 1955 24 Hours of Le Mans. (British Sports Car Hall of Fame)

put his car in the path of Alfonso de Portago's Ferrari 625LM, which struck him hard, knocking out two of the factory D-types within the opening minutes of the 24 hour race. Although the experienced Hawthorn and Bueb were still accumulating mileage, fuel line problems forced the car into the pits for repairs, placing them hopelessly out of contention.

On the bright side, there were still other D-types on the track, among them an ex-works example that had been sold to the Ecurie Ecosse racing team from Edinburgh, Scotland. Piloted by experienced drivers Ninian Sanderson and Ron Flockhart, this privateer entry managed to defeat the formidable factory teams sponsored by Aston Martin and Ferrari, which finished in second and third place overall, barely in front of another privately owned D-type fielded by the Equipe National Belge.

Having won the fabled contest three times in only four years, Jaguar retired from motor racing at the end of 1956 to focus on production cars. Browns Lane continued to support privateers, however, accounting for the appearance of five such entries at the 1957 24 Hours of Le Mans, consisting of two former works cars and three customer cars. As before, the D-type proved almost invincible, taking the first four overall positions ahead of a single Ferrari 315S, which itself finished only one lap ahead of yet another D-type driven by Hamilton and Masten Gregory. It was the marque's high water marque at the fabled track, and closed the book on an era that racing historians described as 'the Jaguar years'.

Bibliography

Appleton, John, *The Jaguar XK-Series* (New York: Doubleday & Company, 1967).

Buckley, Martin, *Jaguar: Speed and Style* (Somerset: Haynes Publishing, 2002).

Clarke, R. M. (Compiler), *Jaguar XK120, 140 & XK150 Gold Portfolio: 1948–1960* (Surrey: Brooklands Books).

Clausager, Anders Ditlev, *Jaguar XK120: In Detail* (Devon: Herridge & Sons, 2006).

Cook, Michael, *Illustrated Jaguar Buyer's Guide* (Osceola: Motorbooks International, 1996).

Dugdale, John, and Michael Cook, *Jaguar Cars in America; The Continuing Story into the 21st Century* (Tucson: Aztex, 2001).

Fendell, John, 'What's the Matter with England?', *Automobile Quarterly*, 10 (1972) 18–33.

Freeman, John Wheelock, *Sports Cars* (New York: Random House, 1955).

Harvey, Chris, *The Jaguar XK* (New York: St. Martin's Press, 1978).

Lord Montagu of Beaulieu, *Jaguar – A Biography* (London: Cassel & Company, 1961).

Lyons, Peter, *Jaguar – Performance and Pride* (Lincolnwood: Publications International, 1991).

Markmann, Charles Lam, and Mark Sherwin, *The Book of Sports Cars* (New York: G. P. Putnam's Sons, 1959).

Nikas, John, *Rule Britannia – When British Sports Cars Saved a Nation* (Philadelphia: Coachbuilt Press, 2017).

Nye, Doug, *British Cars of the Sixties* (Stillwater: Parker House, 2008).

Parissien, Steve, *The Life of the Automobile* (London: Atlantic Books, 2013).

Porter, Philip, *Original Jaguar XK* (St Paul: Motorbooks International, 2003).

Pressnell, Jon, *Classic British Sports Cars* (Somerset: Haynes, 2006).

Robson, Graham, *Jaguar* (Shire: Oxford, 2012).

Skilleteer, Paul, *Jaguar Sports Cars* (Somerset: Foulis, 1975).

Stein, Jonathan A., *British Sports Cars in America 1946–1981* (Kutztown: Automobile Quarterly Publications 1993).

Taylor, James, *British Sports Cars of the 1950s and 60s* (Oxford: Shire Library, 2014).

Thorley, Nigel, *Jaguar: The Complete Works* (Devon: Bay View Books, 1996).

Thorley, Nigel, *Jaguar XK: A Celebration of Jaguar's 1950s Classic* (Somerset: Haynes, 2008).

Thorley, Nigel, Jaguar: *All The Cars* (Somerset: Haynes, 2009).

Wherry, Joseph H., *The Jaguar Story* (New York: Chilton, 1967).

Whisler, Timothy, 'The British Motor Industry and the Government, 1944–1952: A Reappraisal', *Business and Economic History*, 25 (1996) 196–205.

Whisler, Timothy, *The British Motor Industry, 1945–1994: A Case Study in Industrial Decline* (New York: Oxford University Press, 1999).

Whyte, Andrew, 'Sir William – A Fresh Look at Jaguar's Background, A Talk With the Man Whose Idea It Was', *Automobile Quarterly*, 18 (1980) 374–387.

Williamson, Herbert W., 'The Natural History of Jaguar', *Automobile Quarterly*, 3 (1964) 112–125.

About the Author

John Nikas is the author of *Rule Britannia: When British Sports Cars Saved a Nation*, which was the runner-up for the 2017 Mercedes-Benz Award for the Montagu of Beaulieu Trophy. He has published several books on automotive history and is a frequent guest at various classic car events. A regular motoring columnist in the United Kingdom, he is a member of the Guild of Automotive Writers and the Society of Automotive Historians in Britain. He also serves as the Executive Director of the British Sports Car Hall of Fame.

About the Photographer

Marc Vorgers (1967) studied industrial design and graduated on innovative transportation solutions in Arnhem, the Netherlands, before starting his own design studio in 1992. The founder in 2000 of the Classicar Garage (www.ClassicarGarage.nl), which is one of the automotive world's most visited websites, Marc has profiled thousands of vintage and classic cars. He has also contributed photographs, historical information and editorials to publications across the Continent and the rest of the world.